Frank Adloff,
Alain Caillé (eds.)

Convivial Futures

Views from
a Post-Growth Tomorrow

[transcript] ×TEXTS

Frank Adloff, Alain Caillé (eds.)
Convivial Futures

X-Texts on Culture and Society

X-Texts on Culture and Society

The supposed "end of history" long ago revealed itself to be much more an end to certainties. More than ever, we are not only faced with the question of "Generation X". Beyond this kind of popular figures, academia is also challenged to make a contribution to a sophisticated analysis of the time. The series X-TEXTS takes on this task, and provides a forum for thinking with and against time. The essays gathered together here decipher our present moment, resisting simplifying formulas and oracles. They combine sensitive observations with incisive analysis, presenting both in a conveniently, readable form.

Frank Adloff, Alain Caillé (eds.)
Convivial Futures
Views from a Post-Growth Tomorrow

[transcript]

This publication was made available via Open Access within the framework of the funding project 16TOA002 with funds from the German Federal Ministry of Education and Research.

Bibliographic information published by the Deutsche Nationalbibliothek
The Deutsche Nationalbibliothek lists this publication in the Deutsche Nationalbibliografie; detailed bibliographic data are available in the Internet at http://dnb.d-nb.de

This work is licensed under the Creative Commons Attribution-NonCommercial-NoDerivatives 4.0 (BY-NC-ND) which means that the text may be used for non-commercial purposes, provided credit is given to the author. For details go to
http://creativecommons.org/licenses/by-nc-nd/4.0/
To create an adaptation, translation, or derivative of the original work and for commercial use, further permission is required and can be obtained by contacting rights@transcript-publishing.com
Creative Commons license terms for re-use do not apply to any content (such as graphs, figures, photos, excerpts, etc.) not original to the Open Access publication and further permission may be required from the rights holder. The obligation to research and clear permission lies solely with the party re-using the material.

First published in 2022 by transcript Verlag, Bielefeld
© 2022 transcript Verlag, Bielefeld

Cover layout: Kordula Röckenhaus, Bielefeld
Copy-editing: Oliver Vornfeld
Printed by Majuskel Medienproduktion GmbH, Wetzlar
Print-ISBN 978-3-8376-5664-0
PDF-ISBN 978-3-8394-5664-4
EPUB-ISBN 978-3-7328-5664-0
https://doi.org/10.14361/9783839456644
ISSN of series: 2364-6616
eISSN of series: 2747-3775

Printed on permanent acid-free text paper.

Contents

Convivial Futures?
An Introduction
Frank Adloff, Alain Caillé 9

One Step Beyond

**From Lived Convivialism
to Convivialist Transformations**
A Difficult Transition
Sérgio Costa 21

The First Convivialist Steps
Gustave Massiah 31

Feminism and Convivialism
Elena Pulcini 39

Convivialism Facing the Territorial Question
New Spaces, New Times
Paulo Henrique Martins 49

Is Convivialism the Answer?
Depends on the Question
Robert van Krieken, Martin Krygier 55

Convivializing the Economy

Imagining the Convivialist Enterprise
Thomas Coutrot 69

Towards a Post-Covid Economy for the Common Good
Joint Proposal of Representatives of the International
Economy for the Common Good Movement from 16 Countries
International ECG Movement 77

Is a Post-Growth Society Possible?
Dominique Méda 85

Money Creation as a Foundational Tool for Convivialism
Christian Arnsperger, Solène Morvant-Roux, Jean-Michel Servet, André Tiran .. 91

Pluriversalism and Nature

Conviviality to Reanimate the World
Geneviève Azam 105

Convivial Conservation with Nurturing Masculinities in Brazil's Atlantic Forest
Susan Paulson, Jonathan DeVore, Eric Hirsch 113

A Convivialist Solution for the Multiple Crisis of Biodiversity, Climate, and Public Health
Tanja Busse 127

The Post-Development Agenda
Paths to a Pluriverse of Convivial Futures
Federico Demaria, Ashish Kothari... 139

Letter to the End-of-the-World Generation
Débora Nunes 151

(Un-)Convivial Futures

Right Here, Right Now
The Art of Living Together
Andrea Vetter, Matthias Fersterer 161

"2050"
30 Years of Change and Yet No New Beginning
Frank Adloff 175

Once upon a Time ...
There Will Be a Convivial Desire
A Tale in Three Parts about the Possibility
of Convivial Desire, Inspired (at the Beginning)
by Saint Augustine's *De Trinitate*
Alain Caillé 183

A Reflection on 200 Years of Our Youngest Bodily Organ—*Convivialis Futuris*
Susanne Bosch et al. 193

List of Contributors 207

Convivial Futures?
An Introduction

Frank Adloff, Alain Caillé

In 2013, the first *Convivialist Manifesto* (English edition: 2014 [hereafter cited as *FCM*]) was published, initially in French and later in many translations. Since then, many of the social and political problems described in the *FCM* have remained with us, whereas other trajectories are new and unforeseen. This is also the starting point of the *Second Convivialist Manifesto*, which was published in 2020 (Convivialist International 2020 [hereafter cited as *SCM*]). To be a pioneering, public political philosophy, convivialism must succeed in capturing the signs of the times and developing perspectives for the future. As difficult as it is to formulate such positive outlooks, that is precisely what this volume is all about. But let us first take a look at the last few years.

1. Our Times

In recent years, we have seen a strong social and political polarization. In particular, the election of Donald Trump as US president stands out, which entailed a decline in democratic culture in the US. Globally, Trump's presidency challenged many continuities in foreign policy, whether through his willingness to wage trade wars, compromise the importance of human rights, or withdraw from the Paris climate agreement altogether. Bruno Latour (2018) argued some time ago that Trump's presidency represents the first genuinely ecological regime, only under the opposite sign of completely contradicting the idea. For

Trump embodied the clear will to simply carry on as before despite climate change. With his fossil-fuel policy, he abandoned, as it were, the jointly shared and limited space of the Earth. Trump's policy did not care about maintaining a "safe operating space for humanity" (Rockström 2009).

However, the unlimited consumption of resources is nothing new but merely an acceleration of Western hubris and capitalist accumulation, which for centuries has relied on nature as being at human disposal. This is contrasted with another, by now iconic figure: Greta Thunberg, the initiator of the widespread Fridays for Future protests. She has brought climate change to the attention of the public around the world like no one else. Trump's planet knows no limits; Thunberg's Earth trembles under the weight of human beings.

We see such polarization everywhere. While in the summer of 2015 there was still a broad sense of solidarity and a culture of welcome toward the refugees coming to Germany, the mood soon changed and the far-right political party Alternative für Deutschland ("Alternative for Germany") was able to score points with its nationalist and racist platform. It is now represented in all federal state parliaments, and Germany as a country has moved to the right.

Despite the attention given to Fridays for Future, there is now something of a political "yellow vest" factor. Ever since the yellow vests (*gilets jaunes*) took to the crossroads in France in 2018–19 and staged mass demonstrations against President Macron's plans to raise fuel taxes, politicians elsewhere have also feared that any extra spending on climate protection would be another vote for right-wing populist movements and parties. This reveals the current political dilemma: Old left-wing coalitions between parties, trade unions, and the lower classes have broken down, and as long as the additional expenditure for an ecologically 'more sustainable' society is to be shouldered mainly by the lower and middle classes, they can only be persuaded to protect the climate to a very limited extent and may otherwise move to the right. Majorities could only be won for socio-ecological transformation if these classes were also to benefit materially through redistribution policies from top to bottom. These social and ecological questions are closely interrelated—as not only convivialism, of course, has emphasized.

So far, however, there is hardly a country to be found that has rejected the neoliberal redistribution from the bottom to the top. Social inequalities, especially with regard to wealth distribution, continue to increase unchecked, although the voices calling for caps on wealth inequalities and arguing for wealth taxes and higher inheritance taxes are becoming more urgent. Criticism of the capitalist growth economy is also growing louder. When the FCM appeared nine years ago, the call for a post-growth economy still sounded quite exotic or almost absurd in international public discourse. In the meantime, the degrowth movement has become much stronger and more influential across Europe. Many lines of critique come together here: a feminist critique of the economy, an ecological perspective, cultural critique, as well as a critique of asymmetrical Global North–South relations, which continue to be based on (post)colonial, unequal exchange relations and the North externalizing its problems to the South.

In voicing their criticism, many of these movements aim at an extension of democracy and call for a self-imposed limitation in the name of ecology. While the boundaries between classes and citizens should be transcended, new practices of self-limitation are needed at the same time, as this is the only way to guarantee habitability on Earth. The great acceleration in the stress on the Earth system since the end of the Second World War—for example, through CO_2 emissions, energy consumption, water and fertilizer use—urgently needs to be limited, which would also have obvious consequences for Western consumption and lifestyles.

However, many governments and movements are currently opposing the expansion of democracy. In the name of 'true democracy' and the 'true people,' democratic participation rights as well as opportunities for opposition and critical interventions are being massively restricted and so-called illiberal democracies such as those in Hungary, Russia, Turkey, India, and Brazil strengthened. In many countries, we now observe that civic spaces that rely on the freedoms of expression and assembly are coming under pressure and have been shrinking.

The three principles of order of the second half of the 20th century—liberal democracy, free-market capitalism, and a pluralistic and individualistic culture—are currently no longer showing any great stability or attractiveness. In this phase of change, very different paths can be taken. Right-wing populist movements, illiberal nation-states, and notions of homogeneous communities stand in contrast to movements that advocate a deepening of democracy, want to overcome the logic of growth, and seek to reconcile individualistic with communitarian principles. However, the latter can only have an impact if they are able to illustrate to broad parts of the population what more conviviality could produce in terms of positive outcomes for all, including the non-human world. Therefore, the SCM, just like the FCM, tries to develop a language that is as inclusive as possible and to build a broad common denominator for convivialist political aspirations. It goes without saying that this inclusive language has to be reinvented and expanded again and again. After all, reflexivity is at the core of the convivialist program, and this volume is an expression of that.

2. Convivialism during and after the Coronavirus Crisis

The coronavirus pandemic, which began in the spring of 2020, has shown which problematic situations were already virulent: for example, the fragility of financial capitalism, the massive digital and educational asymmetries, or the deepening of gender inequalities through the re-feminization of care work. Added to these problems are the consequences of the current crisis management: collapses in the global economy, newly indebted states, rising unemployment, and so forth. Whether the pandemic opens or closes avenues for convivial reform has yet to be decided at the time of this writing (August 2021). It seems clear that many things cannot go on like they have, but it will be important to draw the right conclusions from the crisis.

One lesson that the pandemic has taught us is that existing certainties can be shattered rapidly and that there is no firm base for eternal business as usual. Delusive certainties have been replaced by contingency awareness. On the one hand, new things now seem possible. On the other hand, it is precisely this loss of illusory security and certainty that scares people. Can this fear be socially managed or, better still, made productive?

In the meantime, it is becoming increasingly clear that the coronavirus pandemic is only the beginning. Compared to the consequences of climate change, dealing with COVID-19 is probably just a minor challenge. COVID-19 shows the different levels of temporality we are dealing with. The fact that many viruses have originated in animals, have been transmitted via zoonoses, and that the loss of biodiversity favors pandemics is increasingly becoming common knowledge. And what if the virus did instead originate in a laboratory in Wuhan, and its release is also part of the story of human hubris? Although the pandemic swept across the world in a matter of weeks, the groundwork was laid by a history of ecologically reckless globalization that spans more than a century.

The virus of neoliberalism, in turn, has been circulating for more than 40 years and has fueled the crisis through privatization and cuts in health care. This shows that the severity of the pandemic has an enormous temporal precedence and that these different temporalities overlap. Now that they overlap in this fashion, similar things will most likely happen again soon.

This is because climate change also leads to acute shocks and catastrophes, be they heavy rains with floods, droughts with water and food shortages, or migration from war and heat zones. The problem of climate change—or more generally, the rapidly changing habitability of the Earth—cannot be controlled. Rather, it will be a matter of interlinking social concepts of time with the rhythms of the warming planet. A critique of the modern separation of nature and culture has long been formulated in earth-system sciences, philosophy, and the social sciences. With COVID-19, societies are now even more aware that this separation is invalid, and the *SCM* itself correctly highlights that there is only one common nature, and humans do not live outside of it.

Since modernity is characterized by a sense of boundlessness and inscribed with ideas of omnipotence and hubris, COVID-19 brings with it the imposition of having demonstrated the limits of this historical path of development. Many social movements from the North and the South are calling on politicians, businesspeople, and academics to abandon the hubris of world domination that the SCM so clearly criticizes. Self-limitation and conviviality among humans and non-humans would have to be considered intrinsically valuable, and one would have to build completely new relationships of meaning that do not negate contingency and interdependence but rather affirm them.

COVID-19 has also made clear how interdependent our world is. It is more evident than ever how all beings (human as well as non-human) depend on each other—even if not symmetrically. Solidarity could grow out of this feeling of interdependence, which was the thesis of the French sociologist Émile Durkheim (1997 [1893]) as early as the end of the 19th century. He related this idea to the nation state; today, these dependencies have become visible to everyone on a global level. But it is not easy to derive a compelling new narrative of progress from this.

One question of the future will be whether fears, segregations, inequalities, and conflicts over resources of all kinds will increase or whether it will be possible not to exacerbate the fear of the future through more individualism and privatism, as has been the case so far, but to mitigate it through more solidarity and convivial solutions. Future hopes for growth, dominance, and prosperity have thus far integrated Western societies, even if these hopes are increasingly proving to be economically unrealistic, socially unjust, and ecologically fatal. Now the task must be to nevertheless develop an attractive vision of living together. Against the fear of losing out to others, new forms of conviviality must be established. It is precisely in response to this that convivialism is trying to formulate new positive answers.

3. The Way Ahead

Convivialism presents itself as a political philosophy destined to follow in the footsteps of the great ideologies of modernity—liberalism, socialism, anarchism, communism. These ideologies are no longer able to enlighten us on either the present state of the world or what it could or should look like tomorrow, if only because they have completely failed to anticipate the environmental crisis and global warming. Convivialism is therefore beginning to find some resonance. The *SCM* has already been translated into six languages. But so far, convivialism has suffered from a major flaw compared to its predecessors, which explains why its audience is not yet broader: It does not 'say' enough. It does not say enough because it does not hold out the prospect of a bright future or at least a happier one for the majority, one that is worth fighting for, or even worth making sacrifices to bring it about. This part of the narrative is what its predecessors knew how to tell. Liberalism gave hope for the rule of autonomy, the end of submission to authority or despotism. Socialism promised equality, or at least a certain degree of equality, thanks to the regulatory intervention of the state. Anarchism trumped liberalism by adding the hope of economic self-sufficiency, of self-management; and communism one-upped socialism by adding fraternity to equality. Convivialism inherits all these promises and tries to combine them by *sublating* them ("aufheben" in German). But this sublation is still largely a conceptual principle. It now needs to be given flesh, breath, life, and visibility. This is the thinking behind the request we sent to the authors of this issue.

Announcing a convivial world for tomorrow might seem both excessively timid and desperately ambitious—excessively timid compared to what yesterday's secular religions such as socialism, communism, or liberal modernization promised us. All of them held out the prospect of a better and brighter tomorrow. We would end all forms of domination or exploitation of man by man. Or, at the very least, everyone would see their material living conditions assured, their health protected, their education sufficiently guaranteed, and would become fully respected citizens. These great hopes have been fading away over the last few decades. Today, for a whole range of reasons (ecological, economic, political, epidemiological, social, moral) that need not be spelled out here, it is rather despair and a dreary future that looms on the horizon. We no longer look to the future full of hope; on the contrary, the horizon of the future has closed. Claiming that tomorrow's world could be more convivial, less violent, less unjust, more secure, more symbiotic or ecological seems desperate and almost foolish.

Nevertheless, the indication of a more convivial future also comes in the wake of the *SCM*. The *SCM*'s main idea can be summarized as follows: Despite the unprecedented progress in the fields of science and technology, the darkest predictions about our own and the warming Earth's future have a high probability of coming true (the coronavirus pandemic does not encourage us to be more optimistic). Our only chance of escaping a dreadful fate is to create a post-neoliberal or post-growth society as soon as possible. The *SCM* depicts some of its possible ecological, political, social, and economic features. However, it is obvious that a convivial society has no chance of coming into existence if a global shift in public opinion in all countries is not triggered, a sort of axiological great transformation. But how can one hope, even for a second, that the power of Putin, Xi Jinping, Bolsonaro, Sissi, Modi, Trump, Wall Street, and the fossil-fuel industry will diminish? Let us remember, however, the strength of the republican ideal, which was able to overcome the absolutist monarchies, the power of socialist or communist (for better or for worse) or fascist (definitely for worse) ideals. Moreover, before these secular religions, there was the enormous energy generated by Judaism, Christianity, Hinduism, Islam, or Buddhism. A comparable energy must once again be mobilized today.

One might say, however, that the rise in influence of the universal religions or quasi-secular religions has taken a long time, sometimes centuries; but now we live in times of absolute urgency. This is true, but our time is one of continuous acceleration: Ideas circulate and passions are unleashed at a speed unimaginable only a few years ago. Often for the worse—but why should it not be for the better?

The *SCM* has presented a brief but reasonable analysis of the situation in which we find ourselves and sketches one possible desirable future. It has been a necessary work of theoretical synthesis. Yet, it is also necessary to be able to speak to as many people as possible and awaken widespread passions for a better future. We are going to need this passion to preserve a viable world. For this, conceptual work is notoriously insufficient. The most urgent thing now is to show as many people as possible what they would gain from a shift to a post-neoliberal and post-growth convivialist future. It would be a world in which, at least in the richest countries, living better means less material wealth, with less money for the wealthy or upper middle classes, and much less exploitation of humans and non-human beings.

What steps are needed to make life better and more convivial? This volume brings together contributions that address this question and attempt to create sketches of a convivial future. This does not preclude us from having a theoretical debate on the status of convivialism or reflecting on dystopias and thus showing the multiple and major obstacles that convivialism will have to face. But the primary objective is to collect accounts of another future world, one that is attractive to an Italian worker, a Spanish peasant, a farmer in Senegal, an inhabitant of a favela in Rio or a slum in Bombay, an Egyptian employee, an Iraqi doctor, a Chinese student, but also one that a French or German company director would be happy to live in.

Whether the future will be more convivial in this sense is decided by our actions in the present, which in turn are guided by the ideas we have about the future. Our bold bet is therefore that convivialist ideas about the future can help decide which future becomes the present.

***

Some of the contributions included in this volume were previously published in French in the *Revue du MAUSS* semestrielle No. 57 (*Demain un monde convivialiste: il ressemblerait à quoi?*); others have been newly commissioned. Our thanks go to the authors for taking on our question, to Oliver Vornfeld for his precise formal and substantive editing, to Stephan Elkins and Eric J. Iannelli at SocioTrans – Social Science Translation & Editing for their English-language editing, and to Karin Werner and Michael Volkmer of the transcript publishing house for their tireless commitment to the cause of convivialism.

Literature

Convivialist International (2020): "The Second Convivialist Manifesto: Towards a Post-Neoliberal World," in: Civic Sociology 2020 (1), pp. 1–24. Available from: https://doi.org/10.1525/001c.12721 [accessed 8/15/2021]. (= *SCM*)

Convivialist Manifesto: A declaration of interdependence (2014), with an introduction by Frank Adloff (= Global Dialogues 3), Duisburg: Käte Hamburger Kolleg/Centre for Global Cooperation Research (KHK/GCR21). Available from: https://www.gcr21.org/fileadmin/website/daten/pdf/Publications/Convivialist_Manifesto_2198-0403-GD-3.pdf [accessed 8/15/2021]. (= *FCM*)

Durkheim, Émile (1997 [1893]): The Division of Labour in Society, with an introduction by Lewis A. Coser, New York: Free Press.

Latour, Bruno (2018): Down to Earth: Politics in the New Climatic Regime, Cambridge, UK: Polity Press.

Revue du MAUSS 57 (2021): Demain un monde convivialiste: il ressemblerait à quoi?

Rockström, Johann et al. (2009): "A safe operating space for humanity," in: Nature 461, pp. 472–475.

One Step Beyond

From Lived Convivialism to Convivialist Transformations
A Difficult Transition

Sérgio Costa

I met Alain Caillé for the first time in February 2014, on one of those bitterly cold mornings typical of late winter in Berlin. I picked him up at a hotel on Spittelmarkt, square in Eastern Berlin. Spittelmarkt is coincidently the address that appears in the professional correspondence of Brazilian historian and sociologist Sérgio Buarque de Holanda when he lived in Berlin between 1929 and 1930 and worked on his classical book *Roots of Brazil*. Originally published in 1936, the book applied, probably for the first time in Latin America, the ideas of Max Weber to the study of modernization in the region.

These topographical coincidences permeated my thoughts throughout the exciting day of activities and conversations. The main reason we had invited Caillé was to participate in a lecture series on contemporary critiques of capitalism organized by a very good colleague and friend, Ina Kerner, who at that time was professor of political science at Humboldt Universität, and myself. The program combined a regular seminar, in which we discussed texts by our guests, and lectures, and attracted considerable attention; some 200 students enrolled and actively participated in the program that had been planned for no more than 40 participants.

Since Caillé had generously decided to spend a good part of the day with us before the evening lecture, we invited him to get to know initiatives in Berlin that could be identified with the ideals of convivialism. The choice was not easy: the city has numerous cooperatives, self-managed cultural centers, post-migrant and post-feminist theatres and even an anarchist party that at that time had 15 representatives in the local parliament: Die Piraten ("The Pirates"). Driven by the campaign slogan "Teilen ist das neue Haben," which translates roughly as "sharing is the new way to have," the party attained 8.9 percent of the votes in Berlin in 2011. Conventional politics, however, does not seem to be compatible with the utopia of absolute transparency The Pirates were aiming for. In the next elections of 2016, the party won no more than 2 percent and lost its parliamentary representation without having left any significant contribution to local politics.

We decided to visit two projects that are quite different from each other, but which are equally illustrative of the promises of convivialism: the Initiative 100% Tempelhofer Feld and the ufaFabrik. The 100% Tempelhofer Feld is a civil initiative that was established to protect an area of 360 hectare located almost in the center of West Berlin where the Tempelhof Airport had operated until 2008. UfaFabrik, in its turn, builds on the name of a legendary film studio founded in the 1920s in south Berlin. Since 1979, the site of the studio has been home to the International Cultural Center ufaFabrik, a self-managed enterprise with around 30 residents and a few hundred other people involved in its activities.

We arrived at Tempelhof field early in the morning and were met by the organization's spokesperson who toured part of the grounds of the old airport with us, presenting the importance of preserving the area in its entirety for ecological, landscape and convivial reasons. Shortly after the airport closed, the runways and adjoining areas were transformed into a vast park. The former landing, take-off and taxiing areas are now gigantic spaces used for cycling, skating, and sailing. The 'vehicles' range from skateboarders hanging from enormous kites and carts powered by sails to more sophisticated constructions on wheels, similar to kite-surfing equipment. The lawns are used for barbecues, improvised football matches or simply as a green beach during sunny summer days, when they are shared peacefully by traditionally dressed Muslim families and young people in beach clothes.

At the time of our visit, the 100% Tempelhofer Feld initiative was campaigning for a cause that seemed unattainable. They were trying to stop, by means of a referendum, the Berlin government's plan to build residential buildings on the edge of the airport site to make up for the housing shortage that has plagued the city. The 100% Tempelhofer Feld initiative, through donations and voluntary work by hundreds of residents, had managed to put together an incredible collection of data and experts' studies, showing the advantages of preserving 100 percent of the Tempelhof field as a park and recreation area. The campaign was difficult but executed with humor and gained important supporters such as the Green Party, which at the time distributed posters with a very unfavorable photo of the then municipal mayor, Klaus Wowereit, asking: "Would you entrust a second airport to this man?" The question mocked the fact that the mayor's main project, the construction of the Berlin-Brandenburg Airport, was promised first for October 2011 and then for June 2012, but due to numerous planning problems and construction errors, did not open until October 2020 and at a cost far higher than originally planned.

The referendum took place on 25 May 2014, together with the election to the European parliament. A large majority of Berlin voters across the city and not just in the areas surrounding the Tempelhof field decided that the park should be kept as it is, with no use of the land for housing construction. However, at the time of our visit, three months before the referendum, the spokesperson who received us seemed to be in a campaign mood. He professionally recited the script he had prepared to explain all the risks associated with the project to slice up the park. Caillé managed to ask a few questions and clarify his doubts while Ina and I just listened. Even so, in the end, if we had not become more excited about the initiative, it was because of the cold wind that pierced our several layers of clothes, prickling our skin and discouraging enthusiastic comments. From a purely argumentative point of view, we were fully convinced of the merits of the claim not to alter the current use of the Tempelhof field as a park. It is worth mentioning that, after our visit and the referendum that decided to keep the former airport as a recreational area, the 100% Tempelhofer Feld movement remained active, seeking to participate in all processes involving the use of the area. Particularly important in the recent history of the site has been the use of the former airport as an emergency shelter for refugees during and after the so-called European refugee crisis of 2015. In this context, new initiatives have emerged and the 100% Tempelhofer Feld movement is now part of a network of civil associations and groups called Wir sind THF! ("We are THF!") and which understands that citizen participation in defining the use of the Tempelhof field is part of a broader project to shape the future. In the words of the network:

> "In the future, the quality of life of all people will crucially depend on how we deal with the challenges of our time. It can only be preserved if climate goals are achieved and democratic and solidarity-based structures are strengthened. This includes measures against discrimination against minorities as well as the successful and responsible integration of refugees and newcomers. Many citizens are concerned with the question of how we can achieve these goals in cities like Berlin and make them sustainable, people-friendly and resource-efficient: How do we make cities liveable places for *all* people?" (Christiani/Saddei/Hanske 2019; my translation)

While driving from the Tempelhof field to the ufaFabrik we exchanged our impressions on the initiative we had just visited. Ina and I also took the opportunity to try to resolve doubts that had arisen in our discussions on convivialism. The first and most obvious concerned the differences between convivialism and other emancipatory concepts such as communicative reason or even radical democracy. In a direct and convincing way, Alain Caillé showed us that convivialism shuns artificial divisions of work and interaction or system and lifeworld. To the contrary: because it permeates across all spheres of social life, convivialism does not recognize artificial cleavages between spaces of coexistence. According to Alain Caillé, a division between certain spaces where instrumental relations prevail, and other social spaces codified by a search for understanding would represent an unacceptable concession to utilitarianism.

Other issues that we briefly mentioned during our drive were more complicated and could not be resolved in the short trip of no more than 20 minutes between the Tempelhof field and the ufaFabrik, even if I, trying to gain more time for discussion, drove the car at the minimum speed allowed along the route. I am referring here, above all, to our doubts about the critical character of convivialism. We were not sure, for example, if convivialism and the anti-utilitarian theoretical matrix that inspires it offer instruments for a consistent critique of capitalism or even for an analysis of power asymmetries in terms of gender, ethnicity, or North–South disparities.

A bit reluctantly, but overwhelmed by the constraints of the agenda, we got out of car at the ufaFabrik's car park, postponing the instigating discussions until Caillé's evening lecture.

It was worth interrupting the theoretical conversation to observe the practical lesson in convivialism at the ufaFabrik. We were welcomed by one of the founders of the project, who since 1979, when the land was occupied, has been following every step of the successful initiative. Without too many adjectives or dramatic affirmations, the founder told us how the group of young people, half adventurers and half artists, who had previously worked together on various cultural initiatives in the district of Schöneberg, gradually settled in and adapted the old film studio to their needs. A permanent outdoor photo exhibition, installed at the entrance to the culture factory, documents and highlights colorful details that the founder, vigorously but in a discreet way, avoided in her account.

At first the members of the project combined all of their incomes. Everything they earned—from shows they staged, from the café, the wholegrain bread factory and, later, from the cinema, theatre, and workshops—were placed in a common fund that was distributed among the participants equally, regardless of the qualification or degree of sophistication of the work done. Even before internal conflicts could undermine the socialist utopias of the commune members, the municipal tax agency intervened. It demanded, in accordance with its Prussian convictions, clear criteria for taxation: if they did not say who did exactly what and how much they received per hour or per month for the specific work done, it would consider everyone to be tax evaders.

The participants in the project have been adapting both to peculiarities of tax legislation and to changes in family situations, as daughters and sons born in the commune questioned the rules concerning living together without formal boundaries. At the same time, negotiations with the municipal government succeeded and the risk of eviction from the land was at least temporarily overcome. Today, the members of the project have a free-lease agreement with the municipality and make intensive use of every millimeter of the almost 20,000 square meters of land: besides the gastronomic and cultural activities, which include the Terra Brasilis Berlin samba group and a children's circus, they run a mini-farm with animals for children and produce most of the energy they consume with a windmill and solar panels. In general, they remain faithful to their founding principle, which they present in a very convincing and coherent way:

> "Approximately 30 residents and over 180 employees come together to live, work, and share their cultural, creative, and social lifestyle with one another. Internationality, sustainability, self-reliance, and self-realization have always been the ideals of *ufaFabrik*, and the way in which members not only approach each other, but their neighbors as well—since long before 'work-life balance', 'networking', and 'sustainability' were the hot cultural buzzwords." (ufaFabrik 2021)

Throughout the visit, an ideological affinity became clear between Alain Caillé, who we encouraged to comment on the notion of convivialism, and the founder of ufaFabrik, whose nearly 40-year experience of lived convivialism seemed inscribed in each of her gestures and accounts. All four of us were clearly disappointed when we realized the late hour and the need to suddenly interrupt the conversation and the visit.

On the way from the ufaFabrik to the hotel, there was no time to return to the engrossing discussions on capitalism and power. We digested the impressions of the visit in unsystematic yet fortunately complementary sentences. The fascination with the project and for that strong woman with unshakeable convictions dominated the atmosphere.

Although we did not address the themes directly, expectations began to build about Caillé's talk and the evening's discussion. Our keynote speaker did not disappoint us. He came very well prepared and equipped for the lecture in an enormous auditorium on the ground floor at the corner of Universitätsstraße and Georgenstraße, with monumental windows revealing passers-by in that part of the city with a rich history. In a clear and fluent presentation, without directly reading from his notes, Caillé spoke for 50 minutes about convivialism, the political context of its emergence, its main theoretical references, and the consequences that he personally drew from the first *Convivalist Manifesto* of 2013 (English edition: 2014 [hereafter cited as: FCM]) and the social movement around it.

We opened the discussion. Participants returned to questions raised in the previous session, when we had discussed, in addition to the 2013 *FCM*, texts from a compilation in German of works by Caillé (2008). The questionings focused on two points. The first point can be summarized as a certain skepticism about the possibility of treating convivialism as a critique of capitalism. That is, the participants claimed that convivialism proposed a world different from the one we live in but without offering a clear diagnosis of the reasons why the world we live in is the way it is. The second point stemmed from the first and concerned the implausibility of a convivialist future. The participants claimed that the project was, at heart, voluntarist, affirming that convivialists seem to believe that socio-economic inequalities and power asymmetries would disappear if humanity so wished. In contrast to this voluntarist version of social change, the participants affirmed that the goal of transforming or even overcoming capitalism cannot be guided by an anti-utilitarian rationality, to the contrary: it requires a coherent project and clear strategies for transformation.

Caillé responded with precision, care, and profound intellectual generosity to each of the questions posed. Ina and I added a few more considerations, but our main points on capitalism and the analysis of power had already been contemplated by the students. From what we added, it is worth highlighting, perhaps, the questioning of the elective affinities between convivialism and other related terms such as conviviality, coined by Ivan Illich (1973) in *Tools for Conviviality* or "convivial cultures," as used by Paul Gilroy (2005) in his book *Postcolonial Melancholia*. Without ruling out possible similarities, Caillé emphasized the importance of maintaining the term convivialism as a noun, to avoid derivations such as conviviality, to ensure the comprehensive character of the proposal and its quality as a movement.

At the end of the public discussion, Caillé commented to us, in a tone both resigned and ironic, that the participants were still too young to understand convivialism. The comment puzzled us. It left us with the impression that the advance of convivialism can only be understood as a mature transformation, above and beyond revolutionary outbursts.

Seven years after that visit which had such an impact on us, and when considering the notes above written for the launch of the Brazilian translation of the *FCM*, some of the central questions we discussed on that occasion remain unanswered—even after the publication of the *Second Convivialist Manifesto* (Convivialist International 2020). The most pressing question is one our students raised in 2014: What is the transformative power of convivialism? Is it really possible to transform dominant ways of life without a radical critique of capitalism? The environmentalist and anti-consumerist critique of capitalism inscribed in convivialism seems to be too weak to confront digital and financial capitalism. That is, contemporary financial capitalism has promoted a concentration of wealth and income that exponentially increases the inequalities produced by industrial capitalism. And this happens in the context of the so-called uberization of work in which labor guarantees are suspended and workers have been stylized as small entrepreneurs, responsible for all the risks as service providers for transnational corporations. It seems, that the quotidian convivial oases justifiably celebrated by convivialists do not have the power to contain and change the old and new forms of super-exploitation imposed by 21st century capitalism.

Another concern that grows with the expansion of the convivialist movement beyond European borders refers to convivialism's capacity to articulate the multiple demands for better material living conditions in the global South. Emerged in societies with solid welfare states, convivialism seems to focus more on the symbolic dimension of sociability. The material dimension of social life is still underdeveloped in the convivialist proposal. To connect with social struggles in the global South, the convivialist movement needs a clear project of income and wealth redistribution, both within national states and from the global North to the global South. Mere declarations of intent are not enough. Proposals for tax reforms and the creation of compulsory transfer mechanisms from the richest to the poorest are necessary.

In presenting these doubts and questions, I am obviously not trying to diminish the transformative power of convivialism. The capacity of self-managed actions and initiatives to transform power relations and re-shape forms of living together at the local level is indisputable, as the examples of ufaFabrik and the 100% Tempelhofer Feld unequivocally testify. The difficulty, however, is one of scale. How is it possible to move from local convivial spaces to planetary convivialism, from convivialism as lived experience at the local level to an encompassing convivialist transformation? How can single initiatives leverage the necessary reversal of the social inequalities produced and reproduced every day and in all spheres of global capitalism? Actually, at least some actors within the convivialist movement have seriously addressed these questions in their effort to enact the desirable social transformations that convivialism has envisioned and inspired. Accordingly, we have recently observed the emergence of various networks including convivialist initiatives in Europe and analogous movements in different world regions, especially Latin America. These new alliances contribute to expanding the social and cultural repertoires of convivialism and to interconnect a variety of local experiences which use different concepts and instruments in their struggles to develop better ways of living together. In the same vein, the current campaign to establish a Planetary Citizen Assembly also points to the limits of conventional politics, focused and confined to national states, for promoting encompassing transformations. We can only hope that these types of initiatives proliferate and are able to articulate local experiences of lived convivialism as driving forces of structural transformations.

Literature

Caillé, Alain (2008): Anthropologie der Gabe, ed. and with an introduction by Frank Adloff/Christian Papilloud (= Theorie und Gesellschaft 65), Fankfurt a.M./New York: Campus.

Christiani, Irina/Saddei, Mona/Hanske, Jule (2019): Recht auf Zukunft. Available from: https://www.wir-sind-thf.de/ueber-uns/ [accessed 8/15/2021].

Convivialist International (2020): "The Second Convivialist Manifesto: Towards a Post-Neoliberal World," in: Civic Sociology 2020 (1), pp. 1–24. Available from: https://doi.org/10.1525/001c.12721 [accessed 8/15/2021].

Convivialist Manifesto: A declaration of interdependence (2014), with an introduction by Frank Adloff (= Global Dialogues 3), Duisburg: Käte Hamburger Kolleg/Centre for Global Cooperation Research (KHK/GCR21). Available from: https://www.gcr21.org/fileadmin/website/daten/pdf/Publications/Convivialist_Manifesto_2198-0403-GD-3.pdf [accessed 8/15/2021]. (= *FCM*)

Gilroy, Paul (2005): Postcolonial Melancholia (The Wellek Lectures), New York: Columbia University Press.

Illich, Ivan (1973): Tools for Conviviality, New York: Harper & Row.

ufaFabrik (2021): The ufaFabrik Story. Available from: https://www.ufafabrik.de/en/14997/the-ufafabrik-story.html [accessed 8/15/2021].

The First Convivialist Steps

Gustave Massiah

In 2002, Stéphane Hessel published *Dix Pas dans le nouveau siècle* ("Ten Steps into the New Century") in which he asked ten authors to put forward their proposals for the 21st century. Twenty years later, we can measure the extent to which unprecedented upheavals coexist with daunting permanencies. It is therefore not a question of describing an ideal and coherent world but of taking into account what can evolve through contradictions. And more precisely, it is a question of choosing the first steps, bearing in mind the thought of Lao Tzu: "A journey of a thousand miles always begins with a single step."

The pandemic and the climate crisis are creating a rupture with the past and opening up a new era. One that will be difficult and contradictory. It will begin with a period of confrontation on economic, social, ecological, political, democratic, and cultural issues. But we can point to some opportunities that could strengthen and renew convivialist proposals.

To appreciate the possibilities for the future, we must start from this new world that is emerging, still finding its way, and resisting conservatism and reactionism. To do this, we can begin with the movements that are leading to emancipation. Among these movements are those to advance women's rights, to solve the ecological crisis, to rein in digital technology and biotechnology, to defend migrants' rights, to protect indigenous peoples, to continue the ongoing process of decolonization, and to reject racism. Each of these movements provokes violent reactions from some corners of society. Their proposals offer new pathways to inspire convivialism.

1. Transitions

In this contradictory period of a world under reconstruction, there are advances that have been made, changes that have been initiated, and avenues that remain open. We assume that in each of the areas of transition, the period to come will see some changes being made while others will still be seeking their path or are only just being sketched out.

Interdependence

Despite the confinement and isolation that we have experienced during the pandemic, what is needed is an awareness of interdependence, of the fact that we depend on each other. There have been new reflections on the meaning of work, on useful work, on essential activities. Health policy is no longer subordinate to economic activity and production. Caregivers and hospitals have raised awareness of the paradigm and philosophy of care. This paradigm concerns humans but it can also be extended to nature, as Enzo Traverso points out. These are openings that, despite the resistance they provoke, initiate the advance towards a convivialist outlook.

A Passion for Equality and Freedom

The challenge to the cultural hegemony of neoliberalism was based on the rejection of inequality and discrimination in all its forms. The passion for equality has not been directed towards egalitarianism. The quest for equality reinforces the defense and deepening of individual and collective freedoms and solidarity. New concepts have emerged in relation to individual property and the monopoly of the economy, to the predominance of corporations, to sacralized consumption. New notions are emerging: common goods, *buen vivir* ("living well/good living"), social and collective property, the democratization of democracy.

Equal Access to Fundamental Rights

The other realization concerns the limits of the market, and particularly of the global market, in terms of its ability to regulate economies and societies. An awareness of such limits should call into question the hegemonic role of neoliberal globalization and the capitalist market in determining activities and organizing the world. What is advancing are claims to fundamental rights and equal access to these rights. The main contours of a convivialist policy are thus beginning to emerge: access to the right to healthcare, to income, to work, to housing and territory, to education, to culture. And also, the right to environmental protection. These rights are expressed at different levels, from local to global. It is the public services—local and territorial, national, and global public services—that enable access to rights. Convivialism can emphasize global public goods and propose to organize global public services.

The Ecological and Climate Crisis

The awareness of the ecological crisis, now that it has exposed the limits of productivist growth, has profoundly modified the very notion of the economy. It has confirmed and modified the perception and centrality of the social question toward the need to combine the social dimension and the ecological dimension. The rejection of productivist growth has transformed the forms of production, starting with energy and transport, and facilitated solidarity-based localization, emphasizing ecology and territorial autonomy starting at the local level. This awareness has led to reconsidering the traditional approach to the domination of nature by humankind, abandoning the notion of infinite time, and reflecting on the limits of human dominance. Society has remembered the role of the pandemic and the climate in the fall of the Roman Empire. The collapse of a civilization opens up long and contradictory periods of transition. New values and new social relationships develop over time. What some people today call collapse can also be a period of emergence of a new civilization. It is not the end of the world.

From Local to Global

Where can convivialism lead us in organizing the world? It is a question of redefining the interrelations between scales, from local to global. The pandemic and the climate have shown that the main problems facing humanity are global ones. And yet the responses have been provided at the national level, by the states. Overcoming this situation requires initiating new articulation across territorial scales. The local level will become the starting point, and communalism will link the territories, the populations with all their diversity, and the local institutions. According to Miguel Torga's (1986; my translation) beautiful formula, "the universal is the local minus the walls." The right to the city becomes a right to the territory that links the rural and the urban. The balance of territories replaces metropolization.

The national level remains a frame of reference. It links history, cultures, and territories. But identity cannot be reduced to national identity; Edouard Glissant and Patrick Chamoiseau's proposal of multiple identities, which are the result of diversity and express the singularity of each person, must be implemented. Unity builds on respect for multiple identities.

Geopolitics will have been recomposed. After a period of displacement of the centre of the world towards the Pacific, the rise in power of Asia and then Africa will have rebalanced the power dynamics between the continents and contributed to facilitating the transition towards a multipolarity that leaves room for balance and equality in the relations between countries. The large geo-cultural regions are spaces of environmental and of geopolitical balances. The sixteen geo-cultural regions will provide the cultural and political support for the international arena: the three Asias, the four Africas and the Middle East, the four Americas and the Caribbean, the four Europeans and Oceania. Globalization will be giving way to globality. The planetary dimension will be making itself felt. The United Nations will be responsible for ensuring the prohibition of wars and arms control. It will be profoundly renewed with two chambers, one in which the states are represented, the other formed from a representation of the peoples of the world.

The democratic imperative

The democratic issue is the most central and the most difficult. It is a question of linking local democracy, national democracy, and global democracy. Three major advances will be made. The first advance is based on the rejection of the corruption that undermines democracy and is the reason for the rejection of politics. It involves breaking the fusion between the political class and the financial class, which undermines politics and results in the mistrust of all citizens towards politicians and politics. Progress towards a balance of power between politics and economics is a priority. An international tax system must do away with tax havens and allow for the establishment of balanced, non-competitive tax regimes. The second step forward is a cultural one. It concerns the redesign of politics based on the refusal of young people to accept traditional forms of representation and delegation. It is about how to combine direct democracy and representative democracy. The third advance is the complete rejection of racism and discrimination. The awareness of the importance and presence of colonization, slavery, and caste systems shows that they prevent the recognition of diversity and the unity of societies necessary for democracy. This implies a long road of constructing the necessary decoloniality for the invention of new forms of democracy.

2. The Convivialist Utopia

Having explored the opportunities that seed convivialism, how do we address the specific changes that convivialism proposes? To move beyond the first steps, we need to resort to a little utopia. Let us project ourselves into a desirable future.

What convivialism proposes is to go beyond hubris, excess, the endless addiction to the appropriation of ever more wealth and the control of ever more power. How can we build a new world without a radical change of mentality, without the discovery of new ways of living together?

Let us imagine that research has shown that hubris is a contagious disease. Not everyone can be cured of it, but everyone can be affected by it. For the addiction to wealth, the cure is a matter of fighting inequality. A general minimum income has been introduced, and the different countries have embarked on a path toward convergence based on a shared global tax system. Taxation is now based on raw materials and greenhouse gas emissions and ecological degradation, particularly climatic. The disappearance of tax havens and the control of banking systems has made it possible to establish equitable taxation. The reference point for this is the marginal tax rates for very high incomes that had been in place from 1933 until 1980. As for addiction to power, a law has prohibited those suffering from the most acute forms of hubris to exercise any form of executive authority.

Other forms of recognition have made their way without falling into mandatory or conspicuous humility. Excellence has not been reserved for individual competition. The emphasis has shifted from praising the best individual to praising the best team. The criterion of success has not been the biggest asset for shareholders, entrepreneurs, sportsmen, or singers. Culture and sport reject elitism and degradation. We have learned to separate success and risk-taking from possession. The commons have made it possible to reinvent forms of ownership based on social property and the public good. Public action has been differentiated from forms of private commerce and state control.

The new cultures have made it possible to overcome uniformity via a diversity of paths. Society or rather societies have learned to value diversity. The balance sought between the individual and the collective has made it possible to find the proper relation between individual freedoms and collective projects. The path is that of democracy, of its constant exploration and (re)invention. In his *Discourse on colonialism*, Césaire (1955 [1950]: 19; my translation) wrote in relation to colonization and the claim of Western superiority: "I systematically praise our old black *civilizations*: they were *courteous civilizations*." This was in contrast to brutal civilizations built on force and humiliation. The search for convivial forms is the way to a new courteous civilization. Convivialism is the antidote to *hubris*.

Literature

Césaire, Aimé (1955 [1950]): Discours sur le colonialisme, Paris: Présence Africaine.
Hessel, Stéphane (ed.) (2002): Dix Pas dans le nouveau siècle, Paris: Seuil.
Torga, Miguel (1986): L'universel, c'est le local moins les murs: Trás-os-Montes, Bordeaux: William Blake.

Feminism and Convivialism

Elena Pulcini

1. Which Affinities Exist between Feminism and Convivialism?

A quick glance at the fundamental theses of the *Second Convivialist Manifesto* (Convivialist International 2020 [hereafter cited as *SCM*]) suffices to note the affinity, or at least the convergence, with the concepts and proposals of feminist thinking. Both are radical perspectives that start from a critical and deconstructive perspective on Western and modern civilization and its pathologies and then draw alternative scenarios and outline, as the *SCM* (3) puts it, "the contours of the other possible world." This echoes a nice and fitting expression by Lea Melandri in which she sums up the objective of the women's movement: "modifying the self and modifying the world." This is no simple task, especially today, in a global world that not only seems to have lost, with the fall of the myth of progress, all faith in the possibility of the better but is also crisscrossed by regressive dynamics. These seem to upend the achievements we thought we had attained: from democracy to equal opportunities, from freedom to the right to a future.

The convergence between convivialism and feminism also seems to hold up against further differentiations within the concept of feminism itself: If it is true that there is not just one feminism but that there are in fact many strands, sometimes very different from each other, it is also true that in each of these strands we can identify some themes and problems common to convivialism. That alone is enough to enter into the diagnosis and start from what is the fundamental and central problem denounced by the *SCM*, namely, hubris—this excess, the *mother of all threats*, in which the origin of the pathological drifts of our civilization lies; this unlimited character that denotes the human being, but which in its extreme drifts leads first to the hegemony of utilitarian individualism and then to the perverse and destructive effects of speculative neoliberal capitalism, whether it is the absolute priority of economics and profit over any other principle or value or the mutual violence between human beings.

It is not difficult to see here the convergence with what is perhaps the heartbeat of feminism, that is, the critique of the modern subject: an autonomous, self-sufficient and egocentric Cartesian subject who defines himself in opposition to a devalued and hierarchically inferior alterity (be it the body or nature, the emotions or the feminine)—a subject, I must add, that in its *Hobbesian* and anthropological-social variations is described as an acquisition-oriented Prometheus, a selfish and instrumental *homo economicus*, an expression of boundless and aggressive individualism, aiming only at the pursuit of his own interest.[1]

However, what is distinctive about the feminist approach to this issue (even in relation to other voices of critical thought) is the conviction that these characteristics are not neutral and universal but rather the fruit, in addition to modern rationalism, of the *masculine and patriarchal culture* that has imposed its hegemony since its Hellenic origins and that must be challenged in its pretention to be neutral.

Thus, what the *SCM* calls the necessary "control of hubris" requires a radical operation of rediscovery and reconstruction of the self by highlighting aspects repressed or devalued by rationalist and patriarchal culture such as vulnerability and dependence, an approach that appears in the work of Nussbaum (2001) to Kittay (1999), from the Italian thought of difference to the theories of care, the opacity of the self (Butler 2005; Botti 2009), and hybridization with multiple forms of otherness (the postmodern feminism of Haraway [1991 [1985]] and Braidotti [2014]). In a word, it is necessary to think of a *subject in relation*, a concept

---

[1] I addressed these themes in my book *The Individual without Passions: Modern Individualism and the Loss of Social Bond* (2012).

that is transversal to the various feminisms—in other words, a subject that is situated on a terrain that is opposed to both the hierarchical separation of the *res cogitans* and the solipsism of *homo economicus* such that it recognizes in the other, taken in its multiple forms, a constitutive dimension of the self.

It goes without saying that this last aspect is already inherent in the convivialist proposal when, against utilitarian individualism and the ideology of exchange and the market, it promotes the value of the bond, reviving a Maussian culture of giving and reciprocity. Indeed, to make just a brief parenthetical aside, it would be desirable that women, often too burdened by the legitimate concern of not reverting to punitive images (devotional and altruistic), welcome, to a greater extent than they seem to want to do, the fruitful novelty of this perspective, which has nothing to do with the sacrificial constraints of this image. However, feminism's emphasis on the *faults* of patriarchy and the critique of the neutral subject adds an element that can, even through that aura of *departure from oneself* that marked the beginning of the first phase in the 1970s (the feminism of difference, from Irigaray to Muraro to Cavarero), initiate a process of unveiling, in which lies in my opinion its most valuable contribution, that is, the capacity *to uncover the most hidden and apparently natural forms of domination*.

I will try to give two particularly significant examples. The first is the rediscovery of the value of care, which occupies a large part of what we can call the second phase of feminism, starting with Carol Gilligan's *In a Different Voice* (1982), in which the need emerges to move from the pure denunciation of oppression and the conflicting demand for difference to the desire to find new words to *express difference* and to fill it with new content, to construct another identity and even a different ethic. Starting from the denunciation of the abstract rationalism of the ethics of justice and rights (Rawls 1971), feminism establishes a new ethical paradigm based on care, inspired by the aforementioned values of interconnection and affectivity, interdependence, and vulnerability. But all this is possible, according to the theorists of the ethics of care (from Gilligan [1982] to Tronto [1994], from Kittay [1999] to Held [2006], from Sandra Laugier [2009a] to Fabienne Brugère [2014], to myself, Pulcini [2013a]), on the sole condition that the notion of care itself is rehabilitated. This means to remove it from the traditional patriarchal image, which, while apparently celebrating its qualities, reduces it to the stereotype of a sacrificial altruism that *by its very nature* characterizes women (frozen in the image of wife and mother) and confines care to the private sphere. In fact, what is hidden behind a positive value is oppression that is even more difficult to reveal. By separating care from this stereotype, women's thinking today demonstrates instead the extraordinary potential of care not only in the context of the public sphere, from which it has always been excluded, but also in its capacity to become a new and revolutionary "form of life" (Laugier 2009b or Jaeggi 2018)—a form of life capable of effectively combating the triumph of neoliberal capitalism if, as Joan Tronto (2013) has recently proposed, it is recognized as the essential value that democracy, increasingly dismissed by the tyranny of the economy and emptied of its *ethos*, needs today in order to begin a process of regeneration that transforms the way we think and love, feel and interact, imagine and plan.

And it is obviously in this sense—the result of a laborious effort of deconstruction and reconstruction that feminist thought pursues as a work in progress—that convivialism can today recognize care as a necessary element of a convivialist society: one that seems to be at the basis of the five principles (in particular, *common humanity* and *common sociality*) on which to institute the control of hubris.

A second significant example of feminism's capacity to reveal the most hidden forms of domination concerns the ecological crisis. This problem is increasingly serious and urgent, so much so that the SCM recognizes it, even in relation to the first manifesto, as unprecedentedly central, inserting among its five principles that of *common naturalness*, on grounds of the recognition that we are part of nature and that we are putting our own lives at risk if we do not take care of it.

The ecological crisis (from global warming to the depletion of finite resources to the loss of biodiversity) is undoubtedly the perverse fruit of this mad plundering of nature that has been perpetrated—especially in recent decades—by a predatory capitalism that is increasingly blind to the consequences of its development model, which today is paradoxically leading to the likely destruction of humanity and the planet. And if it is true that its roots lie in hubris, as the SCM rightly suggests, it is also true, as some feminist voices do not hesitate to point out, that in this case it is this particular variation of hubris that is *anthropocentrism*—that is to say, this vision of the world is entirely inscribed into the patriarchal culture that constitutes, with very rare exceptions, all Western thought. It legitimizes as natural a sovereignty of the human behind which once again is hidden the patriarchal male domination over the non-human world.

This is a truth that women had already expressed in the 1960s and 1970s in the hitherto little-known and ultimately emergent trend of thought known as *ecofeminism*,[2] in which the critique of anthropocentrism is paralleled by the recognition of a profound affinity between the different forms of domination inherent in patriarchal power (androcentrism), ranging from patriarchal domination of and violence against women and domination over nature, animals, and the environment. This clearly brings women's struggle closer to the ecological struggle for caring for the planet and for life (Battaglia 1997). This proximity is also manifest in the recent reflections of Donna Haraway (2016: 67), who in her book *Staying with the Trouble* accuses anthropocentrism of having led us to have to "liv[e] on an damaged planet" and hopes for a radical overcoming of it by creating new alliances, or rather *kinships*, between human and non-human otherness, because "we are humus, not Homo, not anthropos" (ibid.: 55), and therefore involved in networking forms of life that link us to other elements of the biosphere, such as the Earth to which we as humans belong.

---

2 The term was coined in 1974 by Françoise d'Eaubonne, but the movement dates back to the 1960s and now seems to be experiencing a renaissance in the face of the ecological challenge.

2. The Ambivalence of the Relation of the Sexes and the Emotional Revolution

It is true, however, that the convergence between feminism and convivialism finds a limit and a moment of interruption each time the *conflict* between the sexes once again becomes a priority and a necessity in a society still far from real equality. This is because it pushes women each and every time to a legitimate and collective self-defense, inevitably hindering the construction of a project of sharing and cooperation with the other sex. This happens when patriarchal domination comes back surreptitiously or violently to reimpose itself behind and/or despite the proclaimed universal values of liberalism and democracy. And it is not just a question of the phenomenon of a persistent and silent devaluation and violation of the principle of equal opportunities, such as when, in all sectors of public and professional life, and despite their many achievements, women still do not manage to break through the *glass ceiling* that prevents them from obtaining positions of leadership or power that always seem to be reserved for men or when delays and ambiguities accumulate in family law and so forth.

Unfortunately, these are also regressive phenomena in which forms of male violence and oppression resurface, which we thought we had overcome. We see a sad and worrying confirmation of this in the contemporary landscape, where male violence comes to affect not only the dignity and freedom of women in our advanced societies but their very existence (understood as security and survival): femicide, stalking, and sexual harassment are the signs of a new assault on the female body that even requires new words to express it. In fact, we are not witnessing the pure and brutal return of old forms of violence but rather new phenomena rooted in reactive and vengeful feelings towards an emancipation only recently digested.

The proof of this is the spread of the "sad passion of resentment" (Pulcini 2013b) among men who may be willing to tolerate women's professional and social freedom but not their emotional autonomy, their right to deny them, to not love them (anymore); men who know how to exploit women's longstanding emotional dependence by addressing their atavistic feelings of guilt and lack of self-esteem. It is when this phenomenon becomes collective and dangerously widespread that the alliance between the sexes is disrupted and the enemy becomes internal again, no longer clearly defined by a barrier of separation—such as that between rich and poor, capitalist and worker, privileged and marginalized—but within that same relationship of closeness in which love, companionship, and *philia* also exist (or should exist). Therefore, the collective response of women—who have long since learned that their revolution can only be permanent, which forces them to revive the spirit of struggle each time in order to reconstitute themselves as an antagonistic *political subject*—unfortunately becomes inevitable and very legitimate. We need only think here of the most recent forms of organization and protest such as #MeToo and NonUnaDiMeno (NUDM), which have also become points of reference for other movements (rooted in class, race, gender, or religion) and their demand for justice, thanks to the awareness of the intersectionality between the different forms of domination and discrimination.

But the struggle for justice, rights, and equity is not enough if it is not accompanied by the struggle for recognition (Honneth 1995 [1992]), which, in the case of the relationship between the sexes, plays out not only at the level of rights but also at the level of the *personal* relationship with the other and is all the more challenging as women have to confront the ambiguous double face of the enemy/friend of the male counterpart. It is a struggle that requires women to adopt other and different strategies, such as the courage to break through the wall of silence, fear, and guilt and to regain possession not only collectively but also *individually* of their own truth in the covert and crucial context of intimate and daily life. It is a struggle that presupposes women working on themselves in order to dismantle the self-destructive passions and the stereotypes that have been internalized for centuries—to learn, through emotional dynamics and confrontation with the opposite sex in the different spheres of existence, to break free of the tyranny of an imaginary that has often seen them as involuntary collaborators and to affirm their own dignity every time. In the end, it would be a question of recovering the deep meaning of this golden slogan of feminism—*the per-*

sonal is political—by enriching it today with the awareness that we must work on our passions, our myths, our symbols, our fantasies in order to be able to achieve this transformation of the self without which there can be no transformation of the world.

It is clear, however, that this tiring and never-ending work can only succeed if men also adopt it themselves, perhaps—why not?—by accepting the feminist practice of *starting with oneself* and confronting the deep passions that have always animated the patriarchal imaginary so as to understand and change not only its legal and political forms but also the mentality, the culture, the sensibility that guide their own lives and their relationships. In other words, the personal only becomes political when it does not avoid that necessary process of self-transformation that requires first of all to "cultivat[e]," to quote Martha Nussbaum (2015: 2 et passim), our passions in order to distill their empathetic and cohesive essence. I would say that the invitation that convivialism extends to humanity to follow the Maussian recommendation to "oppose one other without slaughter" (Mauss 1966 [1925]: 80) goes in this direction—that is to say, the invitation to adopt a principle that allows us to move from violence to conflict, thus reopening the space for mutual recognition of respective differences and avoiding the danger of their degeneration into inequalities. It is a valuable invitation, rarely accepted by critical thinking, to value the emancipatory quality of conflict and the capacity to manage it in order to prevent and control violence. This objective is not easy to achieve and forces us to ask even more profound questions about the forms that this strategy of neutralizing violence can take in the case of gender relations.

In fact, male violence seems to re-emerge as it is fueled by resentment towards women's emancipation and by tenaciously clinging to archaic images of the feminine. And the female response is restrained time and again, despite achievements on other levels, by paralyzing passions such as fear, shame, and guilt. The project of a convivialist society therefore requires the development of strategies not only to guarantee rights and justice but also to act on the affective life. This begins with an awareness of the traps that lie in the imaginary and the passions, in the dark and ambivalent dynamics of the psyche, which can unfortunately interfere or clash with other undeniable goals. It is self-evident that the stakes are obviously very high, given the objective of building, as laid out in the *SCM* (1 and 7), "an art of living together." It might then be useful to introduce into the convivialist project a sixth principle on which to base the willingness of men and women to cooperate in taking care of the common world. It could perhaps be called the principle of *common affective emancipation*.

Literature

Battaglia, Luisella (1997): Etica e diritti degli animali, Rome: Laterza.

Botti, Caterina (2009): Cura e differenza: Ripensare l'etica, Milan: LED Edizioni Universitarie di Lettere Economia Diritto.

Braidotti, Rosi (2014): Il postumano: La vita oltre il sé, oltre la specie, oltre la morte, Rome: DeriveApprodi.

Brugère, Fabienne (2014): L'éthique du "care," Paris: Presses Universitaires de France.

Butler, Judith (2005): Giving an Account of Oneself, New York: Fordham University Press.

Convivialist International (2020): "The Second Convivialist Manifesto: Towards a Post-Neoliberal World," in: Civic Sociology 2020 (1), pp. 1–24. Available from: https://doi.org/10.1525/001c.12721 [accessed 8/15/2021]. (= SCM)

Gilligan, Carol (1982): In a Different Voice: Psychological theory and women's development, Cambridge, MA: Harvard University Press.

Haraway, Donna (1991 [1985]): "A Cyborg Manifesto: Science, Technology, and Socialist-Feminism in the Late Twentieth Century," in: Haraway, Donna: Simians, Cyborgs and Women: The Reinvention of Nature, New York/London: Routledge/Free Association Books, pp. 149–182.

Haraway, Donna (2016): Staying with the Trouble: Making Kin in the Chthulucene, Durham: Duke University Press.

Held, Virginia (2006): The Ethics of Care: Personal, Political, and Global, Oxford: Oxford University Press.

Honneth, Axel (1995 [1992]): The Struggle for Recognition: The Moral Grammar of Social Conflicts, Oxford: Polity Press.

Jaeggi, Rahel (2018): Critique of Forms of Life, Cambridge, MA: Harvard University Press.

Kittay, Eva (1999): Love's Labor: Essays on Women, Equality and Dependency, New York: Routledge.

Laugier, Sandra (2009a): Qu'est-ce que le care? Souci des autres, sensibilité, responsabilité, Paris: Payot.

Laugier, Sandra (2009b): "L'éthique comme politique de l'ordinaire," in: Multitudes 37–38 (2–3), pp. 80–88.

Mauss, Marcel (1966 [1925]): The Gift: Forms and Functions of Exchange in Archaic Societies, with an Introduction by E. E. Evans-Pritchard, London: Cohen & West.

Nussbaum, Martha (2001): Upheavals of Thought: The Intelligence of Emotions, Cambridge, UK: Cambridge University Press.

Nussbaum, Martha (2015): Political Emotions: Why Love Matters for Justice, Cambridge, MA: Harvard University Press.

Pulcini, Elena (2012): The Individual without Passions: Modern Individualism and the Loss of Social Bond, Lanham, MD: Rowan & Littlefield.

Pulcini, Elena (2013a): Care of the World: Fear, Responsibility and Justice in the Global Age, Dordrecht: Springer Netherlands.

Pulcini, Elena (2013b): L'envie: Essai sur une passion triste, Paris: Le Bord de l'eau.

Rawls, John (1971): A Theory of Justice, Cambridge, MA: Harvard University Press.

Tronto, Joan C. (1994): Moral Boundaries: A Political Argument for an Ethic of Care, New York/London: Routledge.

Tronto, Joan C. (2013): Caring Democracy: Markets, Equality, and Justice, New York: New York University Press.

Convivialism Facing the Territorial Question
New Spaces, New Times

Paulo Henrique Martins

The *Convivialist Manifesto* (in its first and second editions) synthesizes some of the most relevant normative and ideological elements of the social sciences for a broad restructuring of the perspectives of our civilization. It advocates a new way of life, that of conviviality, which emphasizes the value of the gift of mutual recognition between people and between people and nature. In this sense, it has an undisputed theoretical, normative, and utopian value. But how can the *Manifesto's* narrative be translated into political and civic actions that increase awareness of other solidary community networks and systems at the global level? This question makes sense when we consider that the pandemic has significantly altered the organization of virtual and face-to-face spaces by accelerating the pace of technical innovation. It poses new strategic challenges to counter-hegemonic movements such as convivialism at different scales: global, national, regional, and local.

1. New Spaces, New Times

The first important aspect that we must consider is that there has been a significant change in our space–time matrix. This change contributes to redefining the territories of sociability, which are the loci of producing meaning. With the new virtual technologies linked to biotechnology and artificial intelligence, we observe paradoxical effects in the territorial organization of human activities: These occur not only within national borders but within the different physical and non-physical boundaries that are created by transnational social networks. On the one hand, the new technologies have helped to bring people closer together and to generate new interactions between the close and the anonymous, the national and the stranger. One only needs to look at the importance of virtual platforms such as Zoom and Microsoft Teams in the context of the pandemic, which allow many people to work from home, thus saving the costs and effort of physically traveling to other environments. But, on the other hand, the reorganization of spaces increases the social distances between the minority of the population who has access to the digital universe and the majority who does not have the financial resources to go digital or who carries out manual activities in industry or services that expose them to direct risks of contamination by the pandemic. Overall, we can speak of territorial fragmentations within national borders that exacerbate social and digital inequalities.

At the temporal level, it should also be noted that the idea of historical progress has become dystopian, pulling the imagination of the future back to the grim period of the present. This change in the representation of time serves to orient the contradictory initiatives of the mobilization of social, political, intellectual, and organizational actors towards the search for better strategic positions, both in national territories and in the new transnational territories. The flattening of time in the current symbolic abyss is reflected in the diminution of life perspectives and the multiplication of moral and psychic pathologies, especially for populations that cannot access wage labor or that are expelled from the labor market. In addition to the loss of all their civic rights, these people must also face the specter of precariousness created by COVID-19, which further degrades living conditions and social welfare policies.

Thus, we see that the effects of these shifts in the space–time matrix on the old and new boundaries of territorial power must be taken into account when analyzing the prospects for the dissemination of the convivialist ideas. How can the international convivialist movement benefit from the territorial changes brought about by the weakening of methodological nationalisms (Beck 2007) that circumscribed cultural and social experiences within the framework of national territories on the one hand and by the emancipation of globalizing and pluralist experiences on the other? From another perspective, we might ask: Does the reorganization of space and time between the face-to-face and the virtual contribute to promoting the expansion of a liberating cosmopolitan philosophy in a global context where neoliberalism tends to instrumentalize tools, platforms, and artificial intelligence for the sake of commercial and utilitarian objectives, thereby diminishing the spaces of formation of democratic publics?

2. Reterritorialization and Delocalization

The inclusion of space and time is essential to judge the emancipatory possibilities of convivialism. The practice of anti-utilitarian global solidarity supported by certain principles such as those proposed in the *Manifesto* requires initiatives to shrink space and time. Today, the convivialist movement has to deal with the unfolding of multiple territorialities torn between the physically present and the virtual. Each of these territorialities reveals a particular way of perceiving the world, sometimes complementary, sometimes not.

The debate on territorial displacement is of strategic importance for understanding how the convivialist movement can generate an expanded subjectivity that values otherness and cultural and psychological pluralism. This reorganization of subjectivities is necessary to counteract the psycho-political agenda of neoliberalism that generates an absolute and flat subjectivity and in which the subject faces only itself (Han 2017). The *Second Convivialist Manifesto* (Convivialist International 2020 [hereafter cited as *SCM*]: 11) addresses this issue indirectly when it invokes global cultural pluralism:

> "[T]he problem all countries are facing today is how to preserve yesterday's aspiration for solidarity within the framework of the nation imagined as multiethnic and multicultural. It raises the question of

the degree of compatibility between ultimate values and different beliefs (or absence of beliefs). This is the question of pluriversalism."

The *Manifesto* also draws our attention to another aspect of the territorial question, that of the violence of neoliberalism on past modes of territorial activity. The territorial question is an increasingly important topic in this debate because the shift of sovereign power from the nation state to international forums dominated by big corporations weakens the administrative, political, and ideological arrangements that have helped sustain the reproduction of national and provincial narratives that have generated collective and individual identities. In this sense, the *Manifesto* suggests that the emancipation of a convivial global society based on an alternative philosophy to the hegemonic model requires:

"The concern to revive territories and localities and thus to reterritorialize and relocalize what globalization has excessively externalized. Convivialism can only exist in openness to others, certainly (in accordance with the principle of common humanity), but also in a sufficiently solid 'entre-soi' to be a source of trust and warmth (in accordance with the principle of common sociality)." (Internationale Convivialiste 2020: 80; my translation)

According to the *Manifesto*, conviviality can only be achieved through openness to others, through the formation of freely constituted councils that "weave the fabric of a global association of civil society" (ibid.: 37; my translation). If convivialism refers to a new philosophy that inspires ethical and political foundations in existing or yet-to-be-created territories, then the strategic value in the convivialist strategy of debating the location of networks, whether they are physically present or virtual, and the cyclical time of their processing must be considered. No doubt, changes in the cognitive, affective, and moral representations of space and time of individuals have an impact on the possibilities of founding convivialist territorial networks that generate languages of communication and the sharing of interpersonal and intergroup experiences of solidarity.

There is a proximity to be emphasized between the convivialist debate and the postcolonial debate on the subject of territory and locality, which makes it possible to build a bridge between the approaches to the crisis in the Global North and the Global South. The second manifesto recalls that "[t]he end of the colonial era and the decline of Eurocentrism pave the way for a genuine dialogue of civilizations, which, in turn, makes possible the advent of a new universalism. A universalism with many voices, a pluriversalism" (*SCM*: 5). This makes a clear commitment to the convivialist value of democracy. It is a question of seeking an experience of democracy that favors a genuine multivocal dialogue, a universalism of different voices that is built "on the recognition of equal rights, gender equality of men and women" (ibid.: 5).

The document also points out that among the dangers to democracy is "this fracturing of the social space, combined with the neoliberal laws of the market, the acceleration of the rhythm in all aspects of life, and de-anchoring resulting from deterritorialization, ruins the sense of social community" (ibid.: 10). These warnings are fundamental in order to visualize the current global tensions between democratization and authoritarianism, so that territorial strategies can be rethought in the production of webs of meaning that allow new associative and solidary pacts to be formed, whether we are referring to the Global North or the Global South.

Literature

Beck, Ulrich (2007): "The Cosmopolitan Condition: Why Methodological Nationalism Fails," in: Theory, Culture & Society 24 (7–8), pp. 286–290.

Convivialist International (2020): "The Second Convivialist Manifesto: Towards a Post-Neoliberal World," in: Civic Sociology 2020 (1), pp. 1–24. Available from: https://doi.org/10.1525/001c.12721 [accessed 8/15/2021]. (= *SCM*)

Han, Byung-Chul (2017): Saving Beauty, Cambridge, UK: Polity Press.

Internationale Convivialiste (2020): Second Manifeste convivialisme: Pour un monde post-néolibéral, Paris: Actes Sud.

Is Convivialism the Answer? Depends on the Question

Robert van Krieken, Martin Krygier

The first *Convivialist Manifesto* (2014 [hereafter cited as *FCM*]) and the *Second Convivialist Manifesto* (Convivialist International 2020) propose a number of values and principles for how people can live together which one can only find appealing. As an intellectual exercise, too, the *Manifestos* are an admirable endeavor, taking us beyond the usual model of individuals or small collections of co-authors writing articles, books, blog posts and the like, to a genuine collaboration across a wide variety of theoretical traditions. Aiming to develop a more or less unified collective voice on the possible contours of a post-carbon, post-neoliberal, and post-growth society, the *Manifestos* manage to turn the ever-expanding discussion of conviviality into an *ism*.

We agree convivialist aspirations are clearly congenial, and consideration of how they might be brought about important and valuable. However, although we agree that a future flourishing society will be convivial, we are also mindful that it is unlikely ever to be purely convivial. This is both because not everyone will want to be, and because it might be that responses to non-conviviality might also have to be unconvivial. The *FCM* (23) declares humanity's greatest problem to be: "[H]ow to manage rivalry and violence between human beings. How to get them to co-operate—so that they can develop and each give the best of themselves—and at the same time enable them to compete with one another without resorting to mutual slaughter." Well, yes, but this is hardly a novel observation, it has been humanity's problem for quite some time now, and a great deal of thought has already been given to these issues. Some massacres have even taken place precisely in the name of solving this problem.

For us, the discussion of convivialism would be considerably strengthened by a more robust engagement with old and familiar problems, to do with evil, conflict, inequality, competition, and power relations. These concerns are not denied in the *Manifestos*, indeed conflicts are recognized, especially inequality and the broader inclination towards hubris, but for us there also needs to be more recognition of the *intractability* of many of these sorts of problems. This has tended to concern *parties of memory* historically more than they have *parties of hope*, but the latter have as much reason as the former to worry about it. Vicious motives and circumstantial incentives to vices, or excessively empowered virtues for that matter, do not occupy center stage in the *Manifestos*. In our view they need to. The philosophical problem is not so much, or at least not only, to establish the virtues of convivialism, but to reflect on its limits, striking an effective balance between it and its opposites, not to mention how it might deal with "the circumstances of politics" (Waldron 1999) as they are and have often been found to be.

Power-relations are various and ever-changing, but they never disappear and they carry terrible risks. It is wise to be aware and wary of them and to think about what may be done to minimize them, both because they are directly threatening in themselves and because where such threats are realized, nothing much else good will occur. Such a warning might seem at once old-fashioned and banal to an up-to-the-minute convivialist, yet it is simply a form of *moral realism* in the sense identified by Philip Selznick (1992: 175), according to which it is "not enough to think of specific evils as problems to be solved or as obstacles to be overcome. Rather, the perspective of moral realism treats some transgressions as dynamic and inescapable. They can be depended on to arise, in one form or another, despite our best efforts to put them down."

And not just *moral realism* but specifically *political* realism is necessary. Politics and the wielding of power more generally are, after all, not just a matter of the ideal ends we should seek, but of conflict, violence, oppression, domination, their consequences, and what might be needed and feasible to avoid them.

These are the sorts of problems that Hobbes dealt with (and witnessed), however frighteningly and however it might today seem onesidedly. They are the problems that many victims/survivors of humanly devised tragedies also put center stage. They are what led Judith Shklar (1982; 1984; 1989) to enunciate as her first principle of political theory: *put cruelty first*, not to enable it, but to face and deal with it.

They also lead Avishai Margalit (1996: 4) to insist "there is a weighty asymmetry between eradicating evil and promoting good. It is much more urgent to remove painful evils than to create enjoyable benefits," and they led that profoundly Deweyite sociologist, Philip Selznick, to worry that his mentor John Dewey had failed to recognize the weight of evil in the world. Since Selznick was very much a disciple of Dewey, he never abandoned the values he shared with him, many of them as Frank Adloff (2020) notes, of a convivialist temper.

Whereas Shklar thought that dealing with evil was not just primary but actually overwhelming, Selznick disagreed. Animated by Dewey, he insisted that the ultimate ambition of public philosophy was to explore the conditions of a flourishing society, but that required prior attention (not necessarily chronologically but axiologically) to conditions of survival. Only with the latter secured, could one raise one's head and one's hopes.

We also cannot help noticing a tendency to caricature liberalism, or at least simply to lump it together with neoliberalism, as though there were no countervailing political traditions concerned with exactly these sorts of problems, rather merely encouraging ever-expanding materialism. We agree with Selznick (1992: chap. 13) that it is both true that liberal safeguards desperately need communitarian (and perhaps convivialist) enrichment, but equally that communitarian and convivialist forms of life cannot do without the safeguards of liberal political and social principles.

There is no real news here, and doubtless convivialists think about it, but what do they think about it, and how particularly convivially do they deal with it? We would have liked to learn what convivialists say to these sorts of concerns, which are old, pre-capitalist, pre-liberal, and may even turn out to be perennial.

Our reservation is not so much that the *Manifestos* are too normative, as Natalie Heinich (2020) suggests—Philip Selznick (1992), among others, has persuasively articulated the argument for a normatively oriented social science—or even that it expends too much effort weaving together philosophical and sociological concerns; Selznick encouraged that too (Krygier 2021). It is more that the *Manifestos*' sociology is not nearly as prominent as it should be. All the convivialist principles are entirely agreeable, and one could not argue with them. However, to the extent that they run counter to how the world actually works, beyond the pursuit of some worldview that will in itself address existing structures of power, domination, exploitation, oppression and violence, even the supposedly concrete policy proposals remain oddly normative rather than practical, strangely disconnected from the real word situations they are meant to be changing.

1. History Matters

And those situations were not born just yesterday. One of the effects of the weight placed in the *Manifestos* on seeking an *ideational glue* to counter neoliberalism, utilitarianism, and the hubristic tendency towards a limitless domination and exploitation of nature, and on developing a new political philosophy that has more chance of animating public opinion, is an almost total present-centeredness.

If a convivialist sensibility is to take wider root, partly in response to the convivialist exhortations, it is important to see and articulate the change being proposed as the latest stage in a long-term process. The energy-hungry and growth-oriented capitalist world we currently inhabit is the product of a variety of very long-term processes, beginning at least in 1450 (Moore 2016). A sense of the weight of history is essential to any attempts to transform the world as it currently exists. There are parts of the *Manifestos* that point in this direction, to the extent that it emphasizes that there already are *real existing* forms of conviviality, and argues for placing them more at the forefront of how social life is understood and experienced, but how they came about is left unanalyzed.

Changes in moral orientation, habits, belief, norms, and values do not happen overnight. It is entirely possible that a convivialist disposition would constitute a return to earlier types of sensibilities and styles of moral orientation that neoliberal ideas and practices have pushed in different directions, but one cannot know that if one does not attend to the historical development of convivialist but also all the related concepts, such as courtesy, civility, civilization, or sociability. For convivialism to flourish, it will be important to understand and be able to explain the ways in which we are all located in process of *convivialization*, what earlier forms of conviviality looked and felt like, how they evolved and how a market-orientated utilitarian mindset pushed those types of convivialism aside—perhaps identifying processes of de-convivialization.

It is at this point—among others—that the work of Norbert Elias (2012 [1939]) on the civilizing process becomes important, and we are a little mystified as to why his arguments have not been taken up in the *Manifestos* and related writings. The problem of how to live together, despite intense competition and profound differences, with as little violence as possible, is exactly what lies at the heart of long-term transformation of human *habitus* and psychological disposition—closely tied precisely to changing forms of interdependence—that Elias termed the civilizing process. If, as Adloff (2020: 118) explains, "[c]onviviality requires minimal civil standards of nonviolence and tolerance of difference," there are many senses in which the concept *convivialism* is not a million miles away from *civilization*.

The history of convivialism also matters in relation to its intellectual origins, which are most often identified as lying in the conception of 19th century French gastro-philosopher Jean Anthelme Brillat-Savarin, referring to the sociability of a relaxed meal shared with friends and family (ibid.: 160 f.). However, its appeal would be broadened if its roots were regarded as lying equally in its Spanish cognate, *conviviencia*, used by Spanish philologist and literary historian, Américo Castro to refer to a period in Spain's history (711–1492) when Christian, Muslim, and Jewish groups were able to live together without massacring each other. *Conviviencia* has a complex and nuanced history of enormous relevance to how one might understand convivialism today. One of the more important observations has been that it has been possible to romanticize the ways that the different religious communities lived alongside each other, as if animated by a spirit of *conviviencia*, when in reality the driving forces were pragmatism, convenience, and the realities of existing power balances, ensuring that *conviviencia* dissolved like early morning mist as soon as those aspects of life shifted, giving us *inter alia* the expulsion of the Jews and the inquisition. As Kenneth Wolf (2009: 81) puts it, "[t]he 'tolerance' of medieval Spain was built [...] not on any collective commitment to be more tolerant but on the pragmatic realities of day-to-day interaction in a world where people were forced by circumstance to cooperate with one another."

This means that as well as identifying the "institutional orders" that stand in the way of convivialism (Adloff 2020: 118), it is equally important to address the social structures and institutional arrangements that convivialism *requires*, something that would need to be added to the Manifestos' concentration on the pursuit of *ideational glue*. Currently the discussions of *conviviencia* and of convivialism run on two more or less parallel tracks with little reference to each other, with the exception of writers such as Costa (2019), Gutiérrez Rodríguez (2020) and Nowicka (2020). *Conviviencia*, as Gutiérrez Rodríguez (2020: 107) points out, was an important reference point for Ivan Illich's (1973) efforts to rethink how humans should live in the world, given that it "also has moral implications as it emphasizes a communal being in the world, one that is tied to a respectful and caring living together," precisely how the convivialism discussion aims to develop the original French conception of pleasurable shared dining.

2. There's More to Life than Marcel Mauss and the Gift Relationship

In our view the discussion of convivialism so far lacks a collaboration with closely related concepts, forms of analysis and lines of argument that engage with related concerns but all together would constitute a more compelling and persuasive intellectual position. Continuing relations of power and inequality are not ignored, but more attention does need to be paid to how they can continue to operate alongside and within convivialist social relations. Thus, for example, a sober exploration of the sources and significance of *mere civility* in a world of distrust, disgust, disrespect and intolerance might augment the realism of convivialist discussions (Bejan 2017).

Again, Marcel Mauss's (1966 [1925]) work on the gift relationship is indeed very rich and suggestive, and the way it can be connected to theories of recognition adds enormously to our understanding of human sociability. However, an awful lot of theoretical eggs are being placed in the one basket, and any account of the gift relationship surely needs to be placed in the context of all sorts of other types of relationship—of power, to begin with—requiring a much broader range of theoretical and empirical reference points. Just as an aside, we were puzzled by the absence of any discussion of one of the more important earlier introductions of Mauss's work, Richard Titmuss's 1970 book, *The Gift Relationship*, where he examined competing models—gift or market?—of how blood donation should be constituted, drawing out the implications for the structure of social policy more broadly. What is particularly important about Titmuss's account here is his emphasis on the uniqueness of blood donation as a type of gift: its anonymity and the impossibility of direct reciprocity make it a gift to *society* itself, and that, somehow, is where the counter-gift then needs to come from. This would constitute a very significant model for the kind of convivialism being pursued by the *Manifestos*.

Sérgio Costa (2019: 27) refers to the "normative bias in favor of 'good conviviality'" at the expense of a consequential engagement with how one person's convivialism can easily become another's experience of inequality and domination. Like civility, courtesy, and civilization, it is important to be alert to the possible *dark sides* of convivialism, harmful effects that far too often shadow the very best of intentions. The clue to understanding the logic and dynamics, for example, of the damage done by welfare interventions into Indigenous families in settler-colonial settings like Australia and Canada is to go beyond asking, "is it welfare or is it genocide?," to come to the realization that they were precisely both those things.

For Achille Mbembe (2001: 110) one can see in the postcolonial setting an "aesthetics of vulgarity" driven by a logic of conviviality, as opposed to one of opposition and resistance, that domesticates and renders familiar existing relations of power, "inscribing the dominant and the dominated within the same episteme." Mbembe observes that the postcolonial mode of exercising power involves not just control, but also conviviality—"the constant compromises, the small tokens of fealty, the inherent cautiousness"—constituting "the myriad ways ordinary people guide, deceive, and toy with power instead of confronting it directly" (ibid.: 128).

The *Manifestos*' "declaration of interdependence" appears to portray it as a state or human condition merely requiring acknowledgement, rather than as a dynamic process in which different groups of people become more or less interdependent in the context of shifting social, political, and economic structures. Frank Adloff (2020: 60 f.) correctly draws attention to the *Manifestos*' lack of acknowledgment of the analysis of interdependence between humans, non-human and objects in the Science and Technology Studies literature (Latour, Law, Callon, among others), but Norbert Elias also places shifting forms of interdependence, in particular the effects of ever-lengthening global chains of interdependence, at the center of his analysis of the civilizing process. The real issue is not *whether* humans are interdependent, but the ways in which we are, and how those forms of interdependence are shifting, for what reasons, and in relation to which other lines of development. Reference to Elias's work would also enable the *Manifestos* to recognize the need to balance becoming attuned to interdependence with the continuing desire for autonomy. As Elias (1995 [1986]: 36) put it, deepening interdependencies "are accompanied with great regularity by specific tensions and conflicts. No group of people is pleased when it realizes that it is now more dependent on others than before."

Costa has also pointed out that the "relational" conception of human sociability lying at the heart of the *Manifestos* is not at all novel, and that there is a long line of relational sociology stretching back at least to Georg Simmel (who also, incidentally, outlined the sociological significance of the gift in 1908), but in particular to Elias, whose critique of the *homo clausus* conception of human identity and his concept of "figuration" has the potential to develop and strengthen the *Manifestos'* theoretical efforts to move beyond both methodological individualism and structural functionalism enormously. Two of the more central authors of the *Manifestos*, Caillé and Vandenberghe (2020), have elsewhere proposed a return to a general social theory as August Comte first proposed, but it was Elias (2012 [1978]) who argued in the 1970s for exactly this conception of sociology—at great cost to his reputation among German and British sociologists, it should be added, given the low opinion of Comte at the time. To the extent that convivialism rests on a particular way of being in the world as well as a world view, constituting an argument for anchored cultural practices in addition to social and political forms, the *Manifestos'* account would very much benefit both from Bourdieu's (1990 [1980]) sociology of *habitus* and from Elias's account of how and why *habitus* changes over time.

3. What Is the Question?

We would like to conclude by observing that for us what makes the *Manifestos* interesting and compelling is that they lie at the intersection point of many different lines of moral, sociological, and political arguments, and the possible connections between them hold considerable promise. Every aspect of the *Manifestos* that we wholeheartedly agree with in turn raises, we have to confess, an array of questions, often complaints about absences and omissions, and problems unresolved in the *Manifestos* themselves. However, there is now a rapidly expanding literature on *real existing* convivialism, and *conviviencia*, that addresses different sorts of questions from the one lying at the heart of the *Manifestos*, engaging less with spelling out a world view, and more with the mutual constitution of world views and situated practical experiences. Documenting and learning from these widely varying experiences of the pursuit of convivialist principles and ideals promises to do a great deal towards achieving them.

Literature

Adloff, Frank (2020): "Experimental Conviviality: Exploring Convivial and Sustainable Practices," in: Open Cultural Studies 1, pp. 112–121.

Bejan, Teresa (2017): Mere Civility: Disagreement and the Limits of Toleration, Cambridge, MA: Harvard University Press.

Bourdieu, Pierre (1990 [1980]): The Logic of Practice, Cambridge, UK: Polity Press.

Caillé, Alain/Vandenberghe, Frédéric (2020): "Principles of a General Social Theory," in: Caillé, Alain/Vandenberghe, Frédéric (eds.): For a New Classic Sociology: A Proposition, Followed by a Debate, London: Routledge, pp. 24–33.

Convivialist International (2020): "The Second Convivialist Manifesto: Towards a Post-Neoliberal World," in: Civic Sociology 2020 (1), pp. 1–24. Available from: https://doi.org/10.1525/001c.12721 [accessed 8/15/ 2021].

Convivialist Manifesto: A declaration of interdependence (= Global Dialogues 3), Duisburg 2014: Käte Hamburger Kolleg / Centre for Global Cooperation Research (KHK /GCR21). Available from: https://www.gcr21.org/fileadmin/website/daten/pdf/Publications/Convivialist_Manifesto_2198-0403-GD-3.pdf [accessed 8/15/2021]. (= *FCM*)

Costa, Sérgio (2019): "The neglected nexus between conviviality and inequality," in: Novos estudos CEBRAP 38 (1), pp. 15–32.

Elias, Norbert (1995 [1986]): "Technization and civilization," in: Theory, Culture & Society 12 (3), pp. 7–42.

Elias, Norbert (2012 [1939]): On the Process of Civilisation: Sociogenetic and Psychogenetic Investigations (= The Collected Works of Norbert Elias 3, ed. by Stephen Mennell et al.), Dublin: University College Dublin Press.
Elias, Norbert (2012 [1978]): What is Sociology? (= The Collected Works of Norbert Elias 5, ed. by Artur Bogner/Katie Liston/Stephen Mennell), Dublin: University College Dublin Press.
Gutiérrez Rodríguez, Encarnación (2020): "Creolising Conviviality: Thinking Relational Ontology and Decolonial Ethics Through Ivan Illich and Édouard Glissant", in: Hemer, Oscar/Povrzanović Frykman, Maja/Ristilammi, Per-Markku (eds.): Conviviality at the Crossroads: The Poetics and Politics of Everyday Encounters, London: Palgrave Macmillan, pp. 105–124.
Heinich, Nathalie (2020): "My position on your position paper," in: Caillé, Alain/Vandenberghe, Frédéric (eds.): For a New Classic Sociology: A Proposition, Followed by a Debate, London: Routledge, pp. 94–95.
Illich, Ivan (1973): Tools for Conviviality, New York: Harper & Row.
Krygier, Martin (2021): "An Ecumenical Sensibility," in: Seters, P.C.M. van (ed.): The Anthem Companion to Philip Selznick, London: Anthem Press, pp. 189–212.
Margalit, Avishai (1996): The Decent Society, Cambridge, MA: Harvard University Press.
Mauss, Marcel (1966 [1925]): The Gift: Forms and Functions of Exchange in Archaic Societies, with an Introduction by E. E. Evans-Pritchard, London: Cohen & West.
Mbembe, Achille (2001): On the Postcolony, Berkeley: University of California Press.
Moore, Jason W. (ed.) (2016): Anthropocene or Capitalocene? Nature, History, and the Crisis of Capitalism, Oakland: PM Press.
Nowicka, Magdalena (2020): "Fantasy of Conviviality: Banalities of Multicultural Settings and What We Do (Not) Notice When We Look at Them," in: Hemer, Oscar/Povrzanović Frykman, Maja/Ristilammi, Per-Markku (eds.): Conviviality at the Crossroads: The Poetics and

Politics of Everyday Encounters, London: Palgrave Macmillan, pp. 15–42.

Selznick, Philip (1992): The Moral Commonwealth: Social Theory and the Promise of Community, Berkeley: University of California Press.

Shklar, Judith N. (1982): "Putting Cruelty First," in: Daedalus 111 (3), pp. 17–27.

Shklar, Judith N. (1984): Ordinary Vices, Cambridge, MA: Harvard University Press.

Shklar, Judith N. (1989): "The Liberalism of Fear," in Nancy L. Rosenblum (ed.): Liberalism and Moral Life, Cambridge, MA: Harvard University Press, pp. 21–38.

Titmuss, Richard (2018 [1970]): The Gift Relationship, 3rd ed., London: Policy Press.

Waldron, Jeremy (1999): Law and Disagreement, Oxford: Oxford University Press.

Wolf, Kenneth Baxter (2009): "Convivencia in Medieval Spain: A Brief History of an Idea," in: Religion Compass 3 (1), pp. 72–85.

Convivializing the Economy

Imagining the Convivialist Enterprise

Thomas Coutrot

There is no need to point out here that capitalism is leading the biosphere into an unsustainable trajectory in the mid-term (10 to 30 years). Greenhouse gas emissions have only temporarily stopped increasing 'thanks' to COVID-19, and rich countries have only slightly reduced their own emissions over the last 20 years by relocating their industrial production to Asia. Industrial animal husbandry and agriculture are destroying the soil and causing pandemics of zoonotic diseases. The concentration of wealth (26 individuals own as much as the poorest 4 billion) exacerbates the concentration of economic and political power in the hands of a technophile elite who rely on innovation and science to achieve green growth. The health crisis, which has further reinforced digital capitalism and social inequality, only confirms these perspectives.

Concentration of wealth and ecological destruction have their roots in the same socio-economic system: the link between the large capitalist companies focused on shareholder value and the financial markets that impose their disciplinary power. The current troubles of Danone, a model of a *mission company* ("health through food") but one that has been forced by its shareholders to cut thousands of jobs to increase its operating margin to 20 percent, are a recent illustration. It is true that (1) many alternatives exist and are developing all over the world under the lead of a creative civil society. But (2) they have only a marginal effect on the trajectory of capitalism, and (3) their change of scale can only come from major institutional shifts that break with the fundamental laws of capitalism.

1. Eco-Solidary Alternatives: Effective and Dynamic but Marginal

Countless surveys show that the digital revolution, far from improving the quality and fulfilment of work, is being used to standardize tasks, control activity, and subordinate it to a *governance by numbers* in the service of finance. Faced with work that at best loses all meaning and at worst destroys the planet, a growing number of workers is becoming involved in experiments, sometimes on a large scale, that show how economic efficiency (the careful use of resources) can be reconciled with ecology and democracy. Small-scale farming and permaculture have a very small ecological footprint but make intensive use of labor and knowledge to achieve remarkable yields. Citizens' cooperatives are developing decentralized, human-scale renewable energy sources. Work collectives are taking over or creating industrial or service companies in the form of an SCIC (Société coopérative d'intérêt collectif) or SCOP (Société coopérative et participative),[1] which combine economic, ecological, and democratic goals. Employment cooperatives (Coopérative d'activité et d'emploi) bring together thousands of self-employed workers to offer them the protections of salaried employment and collaborative work opportunities. Participatory financing platforms are channeling public savings into eco-solidarity projects. Wikipedia's 20th anniversary is a reminder that the takeover of the Web by GAFAM (Google, Apple, Facebook, Amazon, and Microsoft) is neither inevitable nor irreversible and that thousands of collaborative and open-source projects continue to flourish.

In fact, there are few areas—apart from the nuclear and arms industries—where eco-solidary alternatives have not proven their viability, even in today's hostile environment. Yet they still carry very little

---

1   The SCIC, a cooperative society of collective interest, is a cooperative enterprise whose purpose is the production or supply of goods or services in the collective interest that also have social utility. A SCOP is a commercial company that differs from traditional companies in that employees hold a majority of the capital and have decision-making power.

weight: There is no point in celebrating the fact that the social and solidary economy accounts for 10 percent of GDP in France if it is mainly thanks to the large mutual banks and insurance companies and the agricultural or commercial cooperatives, whose behavior is hardly different from that of their profit-driven counterparts. At the current rate of growth of truly eco-solidary initiatives, it would take decades—which we do not have—for them to begin to have a significant impact on the overall trajectory of the system.

2. The Impossible Greening of Capitalism

In the meantime, the global economy is continuing its unsustainable trajectory as if nothing had happened. Despite the Paris Agreement, CO_2 emissions continued to grow by almost 2 percent year on year between 2017 and 2019, fell in 2020 only on account of COVID-19, and are about to shoot up again in the wake of a thoughtless recovery. As noted earlier, the low emissions reductions in OECD countries over the past 20 years are due to the relocation of industries to Asia.

It is true that large companies, under pressure from public opinion and seeking to attract young graduates, who are increasingly demanding an environmental quality to their work, are showing a desire, sometimes followed by action, to make their activity greener and reduce their carbon footprint. The agro-industry is developing organic products but with production methods that are just as damaging as industrial farming. Google, Facebook, and Apple are developing their own autonomous sources of renewable energy to power their gigantic data centers, but their very activity is based on planned obsolescence and excessive consumerism. Car manufacturers are aiming for 100 percent electricity, but battery production is an environmental disaster. 5G is slightly more energy efficient per megabyte transferred, but it could increase the amount of data channeled through the Web by a factor of ten.

It is clear that the emission reduction targets set by the Intergovernmental Panel on Climate Change (IPCC) will not be met. The use of geoengineering, which claims to remedy the consequences without addressing the causes, could progressively be imposed in the name of the need to avoid even worse catastrophes. Sequestration and storage of carbon, injection of sulfur aerosols into the atmosphere, seeding the oceans with billions of tons of iron... the sorcerer's apprentices of productivism have no shortage of ideas—or multinationals ready to implement them.

Capitalism is a system in which investment decisions are made by firms struggling for survival and therefore forced to maximize the return on those investments regardless of their concrete effects on the world. Competition forces the constant creation of new products and new needs, regardless of good and sometimes true intentions or even bold regulations. The *rebound effect* that wipes out the impact of clean technologies on CO_2 emissions is intrinsically linked to the deep dynamics of capitalism. Moreover, the growing concentration of capital—one of Marx's few unchallenged predictions—leads to a concentration of political power in the hands of an oligarchy that is already showing us, even in France, how easily it is willing to restrict or eliminate political freedoms if its dominance is at stake.

Taking these ecological threats seriously, moving towards a convivialist society governed by freedom, equality, and fraternity not only between humans but also with all living beings, obliges us to think about other ways of making investment choices: not by state intervention, nor by suppressing markets—which obviously preceded and will survive capitalism and likewise remain an important condition of freedom—but by redesigning the governance of companies in order to restrict the objective of profit to a secondary and instrumental role.

3. Thinking of the Enterprise as a Productive Commons

To put it in one sentence, it is a question of placing the objective of *taking care*—of health, nature, and democracy—at the heart of decisions on what and how to produce. All the proposals on unconditional basic income and social protection, taxation, money and debt, regulation of international trade, and so forth are meaningless if the logic of maximum profit continues to determine investment choices.

The state must of course develop and democratize public services (e.g., health, education, housing) and money (e.g., put central banks back under political control). But it is not its role to run all companies. Classical industrial democracy (known since the 1970s as *self-management*) is not adapted to today's challenges either, because it makes the workers alone the masters of their company's destiny; but, except in small and medium-sized companies, they are never the only ones affected by its activity. The appropriate model is that of the commons: All the stakeholders directly concerned by a production activity must be able to define together the aims and operating methods of this activity. Eco-solidary democracy should include long-term investors and employees in the process of governance, as well as public authorities, customers/users, local residents' associations, and environmental groups. The SCIC model is perfectly suited for these purposes.

It is therefore not a question of nationalization or state control but of socializing companies, that is to say, placing them under the control of collective deliberation by stakeholders. It is also a question of completely rethinking the modalities of the division and coordination of labor. Instead of the *command and control* characteristic of the capitalist company, we now have methods of organizing work in a nonhierarchical way, such as sociocracy or holacracy, which are based on a careful balance between overall coherence and the broad autonomy of work groups and individuals. Recent innovations in collaborative organization (popularized and sometimes abused under the term *liberated enterprise*) establish loops of reciprocal control between the various levels of organization in the company, which make it possible to think of and implement genuine participation by all in the decisions that concern them, even in large structures, without sacrificing efficiency in the pursuit of common goals. These goals, chosen by deliberation, will not be return on investment but rather a diversity of criteria linked to the social utility of the production and its impact on social cohesion and nature, both of which need to be taken care of.

Of course, this presupposes major institutional transformations as a result of the serious economic, ecological, and political crises we see before us. In the near future, less radical changes in the direction of socialization could be promoted, such as the institution of a right to co-determination of major investment and employment decisions and the inclusion of external stakeholders in deliberative bodies (e.g., boards of directors and/or employee representative bodies).

Establishing the enterprise as a productive commons also presupposes, of course, a rethinking of the ownership of the means of production, either by dissociating *usus*, *fructus*, and *abusus* (e.g., a shareholder will be able to receive dividends without having exclusive decision-making power) or by abolishing their lucrative ownership (e.g., by financing enterprises exclusively through credit, which is itself socialized). It is also important to decentralize the productive fabric (except for natural monopolies such as the railways or the electricity network) so as to restore a convivial dimension to work collectives.

Finally, the decisions of socialized companies must be incorporated into a more global framework of socio-ecological planning that ensures the macroeconomic degrowth, at the necessary pace, of energy and material consumption and the reduction of inequalities. The plan is not incompatible with markets, but only a plan can provide the framework to ensure that the limits of the planet are respected.

Conclusion

The environmental movement, which was on the rise before the pandemic and will certainly take off again afterwards, is of course a major social force in the necessary transition. However, it has shown little interest in the forms of work and enterprise that would allow a real transition. It supports eco-solidary initiatives, universal income, and public regulations but does not make strong institutional proposals to free living labor from the grip of dead labor and allow it to take care of the world. It too often acts as if public regulation would be enough to force multinationals to be socially and environmentally responsible, without touching the deep logic of capitalist accumulation. In France the recent convergence between the environmental movement and the trade union movement, notably in the collective Plus jamais ça ("Never Again"), which includes the Confédération générale du travail (CGT), Solidaires, the Fédération syndicale unitaire (FSU), the Confédération paysanne, Attac, Greenpeace, Oxfam, and many others, is an unprecedented opportunity to move forward on these issues and thus to remove an important obstacle to a radical social transformation as envisaged by convivialism: acceptance of capitalist economic rationality as the only possible global rationality.

Towards a Post-Covid Economy for the Common Good
Joint Proposal of Representatives of the International Economy for the Common Good Movement from 16 Countries[1]

International ECG Movement

The international Economy for the Common Good (ECG) movement, which is for the first time going public jointly with this text, has been proposing since 2010 a consistent and complete alternative economic model. ECG is based on fundamental values—such as sustainability, inclusion, and cooperation—instead of putting financial goals first and privileging competition. The prevailing model contributes to growing threats to humankind such as climate change and the loss of biodiversity—as well as the current pandemic. COVID-19 is only the latest of a

---

1   Authors and signatories: Urbain N'Dakon (chairman, Maat-ECG Africa and African diaspora), Luciana Cornaglia (president, ECG Argentina), Christian Felber (movement founder, Austria), Lisa Muhr (president, ECG Austria), Karla Schimmel (member, ECG Belgium), Silvia Álvarez (board member, ECG Chile), Henry Garay-Sarasti (co-coordinator, ECG Colombia), Gerd Hofielen (speaker, ECG Germany), Lidia di Vece (president, ECG Italy), Marianne Kert (board member, ECG Luxembourg), Luisa Montes (board member, ECG Mexico), Estefanía Matesanz (chairwoman, ECG Netherlands), Debla Orihuela (president, ECG Spain), Paco Álvarez (ambassador, ECG Spain), Thomas Söderberg (chairman, ECG Sweden), Gaby Belz and Ralf Nacke (members of the board, ECG Switzerland), Sandra White (director, ECG UK), Gualberto Trelles (coordinator EBC Montevideo/Uruguay).

series of viruses seriously affecting human health and lives. HIV, Ebola, Sars1, and Mers and now Sars2 are all examples of zoonosis, which means that a virus changes its host from animal to human. There is scientific evidence that the increased occurrence of zoonosis is a consequence of over-exploiting natural resources and growing pressure on wildlife habitats, from deforestation, uncontrolled hunting, industrial agriculture, and air pollution (Shah 2020).

The current pandemic—as well as other threats—did not appear without previous warnings from scientists: *Limits to Growth* (1972), *Brundtland Report* (1987), *Earth Charter* (2000), *Millennium Ecosystem Assessment Synthesis Report* (2005), and the concept of *planetary boundaries* (2009) are prominent examples. This leads us to the question: How is it possible that these warnings have not been heeded by decision-makers on all levels?

1. The Influence of Business Lobbying

In the last decades, lobbying organizations serving vested economic interests have spent a lot of money to capture the Rio-Johannesburg process, to question or deny climate change, to prevent binding regulations for multilateral enterprises—and, most recently, to put a Multilateral Investment Court (MIC) on the international agenda of the EU (European Commission 2016). These interventions are detrimental to nature and basic rights of the large majority of human beings, and they have been undermining democracy.

Consequently, the systemic root causes of ecological and health problems are not represented adequately in the public discourse; media attention is mainly focused on vaccination and products created by pharmaceutical companies. The progressive privatization of the WHO—the private foundation of Bill and Melinda Gates is already the second biggest funder of this body (World Health Organization 2019)—is severely undermining public policies and democratic priorities. A holistic health policy approach would develop strategies to avoid future zoonosis—by improving the sustainability of economic activities, and by fostering people's health and resilience through healthy food, safe employment, social inclusion, and eradication of poverty.

2. Flatten Other Curves

We can learn from the current crisis: humankind has to take a respectful attitude towards Earth, considering ourselves as part of the web of life, neither external from, nor superior to the rest. We need to raise awareness of our own vulnerability and our dependence on an intact environment, creating a respectful co-existence with all forms of life. Endless economic growth has turned into a dangerous risk: scientists have defined nine critical planetary boundaries, some of which we have already exceeded (Stockholm Resilience Centre 2021). With the same rigor and determination governments have shown when trying to flatten the COVID-19 contagion curve, we now need to flatten the curves for land use, energy and resource consumption, inequality, and the unlimited power of international corporations.

3. Towards an Economy for the Common Good

Since 2010, the Economy for the Common Good movement has spread to 30 countries on all continents, where 200 local chapters are active. 3000 organizations support the movement. 700 companies, schools, universities, municipalities, and city districts have implemented a common good balance sheet. Eight regional governments in Spain, Austria, and Germany have included it in their government programs. In 2015, the European Economic and Social Committee published an own-initiative opinion on the ECG model (European Economic and Social Committee 2015), in a second opinion the EESC declared the ECG a "new sustainable economic model" (European Economic and Social Committee 2017).

The ECG is a fully ethical market economy that puts private enterprises and property at the service of the common good—in order to protect global ecosystems and fundamental values, from dignity to justice and solidarity to sustainability and democracy (Economy for the Common Good 2021). The Common Good Product, measuring all relevant aspects of life quality, could sit above the GDP. An economy that puts people's needs and democratic values first and considers money and other forms of capital as resources to achieve these goals, is actually what the ancient Greeks meant by *oikonomía*. Prioritizing financial results is its opposite: *chrematistiké* or capitalism, as we call it today (Dierksmeier/Pirson 2009). An economy oriented to the common good is the only way to leave a healthy and viable planet to our children and grandchildren. The current COVID-19 crisis gives us the opportunity to master this transition.

4. Change the Trade Paradigm

Trade should serve the goal of stabilizing the planet's climate, maintaining biodiversity and cultural diversity, and of protecting human rights, basic needs, and dignity. It should help create the "safe space" proposed by Kate Raworth's "Doughnut model" (Raworth 2021). *Ethical trade* and *economic subsidiarity*—giving priority to proximity and local economies and using international trade as a complement—should replace *free trade* as the dominant doctrine in global trade (Felber 2019). Mercosur, CETA, and other agreements, are clearly examples of the old-style *enforced trade* paradigm with harmful consequences. One example of how such an *ethical world trade order* could be established is a carbon tax of for example 100 USD per ton CO_2, as recommended by the *Stiglitz-Stern Report* in 2017 (Carbon Pricing Leadership Coalition 2017: 3). Countries that fulfil this goal get the right to levy the difference to countries with lower (or no) taxes with an ecological tariff.

5. Change the Tax Paradigm

An urgent and just solution to skyrocketing inequality is a higher taxation of capital income, private property, and inheritances—while at the same time democratizing progressively to prevent corruption and put states in service to the people. In the Euro zone, private wealth exceeds public debt by a factor of five. Higher taxes on wealth would enable needed investments in health, education, poverty elimination and economic transformation. The *financial transaction tax* should be introduced, ideally on a global level. It is a worrying symptom of postdemocracy that this highly accepted proposal for a regulation of financial markets was pushed off the EU agenda, although tax revenues would have amounted to up to 310 billion euros, according to the Vienna-based WiFo (Schulmeister 2011: 33). Principally, the international movement of capital should be linked to fiscal transparency and cooperation, in order to reduce tax evasion and close tax havens.

6. Combine Fiscal and Monetary Policy

As the economic downturn in 2020 will be very steep, joint forces of fiscal and monetary policy are advisable. Quantitative easing is a measure with limited effect—if used to buy corporate bonds, it can even be counterproductive. A combination of Eurobonds (*coronabonds*) and interest-free loans from central banks to the state (Modern Monetary Theory) up to a reasonable cap, would be more effective. Art. 123 (1) of the TFEU, which prohibits direct loans from the ECB to members of the eurozone, should be adjusted.

7. Change the Rescue Priorities

The current crisis management should not repeat earlier failures: in the 2008 financial crisis, we have seen the saving of so-called 'systemically important' entities ('too big to fail'), most of them closely linked to the vested economic interests mentioned before. It is time to break this logic, and focus on what we all need:

- public investment in health, education, sustainable public transport, housing, and sustainable food production, thereby creating meaningful and climate-friendly employment and help transform the economy towards sustainability;
- the introduction of an unconditional basic income (UBI), which is sufficiently high to cover all of a person's basic needs;
- a minimum wage (sensibly higher than the UBI) combined with a maximum income, in view to reducing inequality to an acceptable level and making our societies more inclusive;
- financial or fiscal support primarily to SMEs which contribute to the common good, for example, they are climate-friendly, strive for social inclusion and cohesion and are aware of the importance of biodiversity. One criterion could include an externally audited non-financial report, such as a Common Good Balance Sheet, a B Corps Certification, or a similar tool. We envisage that in the mid-term *all* organizations will have to take on these responsibilities.

We are aware of the scale and huge challenge of the proposed changes, as the current model is firmly established, and many people are dependent on it. Nevertheless, more and more companies, municipalities, regions, and governments are engaging in the implementation of these new ideas and practices. Companies which have started to take social, ecological, and democratic responsibility are winning awards and are receiving support from all sides. Cities like Barcelona, Amsterdam, Stuttgart, and Vienna are beginning to promote these necessary changes. The growing ECG movement is willing to work with more citizens, companies, and governments to achieve these goals.

One Planet, June 15, 2020

Literature

Carbon Pricing Leadership Coalition (2017): Report of the High-Level Commission on Carbon Prices. Available from: https://www.carbonpricingleadership.org/report-of-the-highlevel-commission-on-carbon-prices [accessed 8/15/2021].

Dierksmeier, Claus/Pirson, Michael (2009): "Oikonomia Versus Chrematistike: Learning from Aristotle About the Future Orientation of Business Management," in: Journal of Business Ethics 88, pp. 417–30.

Economy for the Common Good (2021). Available from: https://www.ecogood.org/ [accessed 8/15/2021].

European Commission (2016): The Multilateral Investment Court project. Available from: http://trade.ec.europa.eu/doclib/press/index.cfm?id=1608 [accessed 8/15/2021].

European Economic and Social Committee (2015): Economy for the Common Good. Available from: https://www.eesc.europa.eu/our-work/opinions-information-reports/opinions/economy-common-good [accessed 8/15/2021].

European Economic and Social Committee (2017): New sustainable economic models (exploratory opinion requested by the Commission). Available from: https://www.eesc.europa.eu/en/our-work/opinions-information-reports/opinions/new-sustainable-economic-models-exploratory-opinion-requested-commission [accessed 8/15/2021].

Felber, Christian (2019): Trading for Good: How Global Trade Can be Made to Serve People Not Money, London: Zed Books.

Raworth, Kate (2021): What on Earth is the Doughnut?... Available from: https://www.kateraworth.com/doughnut/ [accessed 8/15/2021].

Schulmeister, Stephan (2011): Implementation of a General Financial Transactions Tax, Research assistance: Eva Sokoll, Wien: Österreichisches Institut für Wirtschaftsforschung. Available from: https://www.wifo.ac.at/pubma-datensaetze?detail-view=yes&publikation_id=41992 [accessed 8/15/2021].

Shah, Sonia (2020): "Think Exotic Animals Are to Blame for the Coronavirus? Think Again," in: The Nation. Available from: https://www.thenation.com/article/environment/coronavirus-habitat-loss/ [accessed 8/15/2021].

Stockholm Resilience Centre (2021): The nine planetary boundaries. Available from: https://www.stockholmresilience.org/research/planetary-boundaries/planetary-boundaries/about-the-research/the-nine-planetary-boundaries.html [accessed 8/15/2021].

World Health Organization (2019): Voluntary contributions by fund and by contributor, 2018 (= 72nd World Health Assembly, Provisional agenda item 15.2, A72/INF./5, 9 May 2019). Available from: https://apps.who.int/iris/bitstream/handle/10665/329246/A72_INF5-en.pdf?sequence=1&isAllowed=y [accessed 8/15/2021].

Is a Post-Growth Society Possible?

Dominique Méda

Since the 2000s, a certain number of people have been defending the idea of a post-growth society. Personally, I acquired this conviction while working on the issue of what exactly a rich society is by trying to understand the origins of the equation between GDP and wealth (Méda 1999). In particular, my colleagues Jean Gadrey, Florence Jany-Catrice, Isabelle Cassiers, and myself as part of the Forum pour d'Autres Indicateurs de Richesse ("Forum for Other Wealth Indicators"; FAIR) examined the possibility of supplementing GDP with other wealth indicators. If I were to use a hypothetical example, I would say that this post-growth society could come about on the condition that GDP (e.g., production) were bound by strict social and environmental limits that might take the concrete form of the Social Health Index (Jany-Catrice/Marlier 2020) and a carbon footprint. These two indicators would likely play the dual role of an alert system and a threshold that should not be crossed—a national threshold that can be broken down by organizations, territories, or individuals.

Some might object that this is a very technical, even quantophrenic vision, giving in to the temptation to put everything in the form of figures and indicators, and that it is not enough to define indicators for society to change as if by a miracle. This is true. However, I would like to respond by reminding you, first of all, of the extent to which the GDP—or at least the system of national accounts, which, you will recall, is universal—frames and constrains our actions and particularly our public actions. It is a real cognitive framework based on a scheme for interpreting the world, a grammar in which it has been decided once and for all what counts and what does not. This grammar was developed in the interwar period and after the Second World War within the context of a number of values and beliefs that were codified in this tool. Simon Kuznets (1941: 5), the man who estimated the US national income in 1934 and again in 1941, was fully aware that what he was constructing was based on a multitude of conventions when he wrote:

> "For those not intimately acquainted with this type of work it is difficult to realize the degree to which estimates of national income have been and must be affected by implicit or explicit value judgments. [...] The apparent relative unanimity produced by empirical writings on national income is due largely to the estimators' unconscious acceptance of one social philosophy and their natural reluctance to face such fundamental issues as would reveal that estimates are conditioned by controversial criteria."

Nowadays, as François Fourquet (1980) brilliantly reminded us in *Les Comptes de la puissance*, we hate degrowth. We want dynamism. We overlook the fact that growth comes with degradation. We want to escape scarcity, rationing, famine, and discomfort. Growth is synonymous with expansion, emancipation, progress, health, and improvement. We have to renew our infrastructure, feed the population, build houses, make cars; economic productivity is seen as the core of progress; consumption is regarded as a necessity and a joy to which all should have access. We are still living within this framework and the mechanisms for valorization created all those decades ago, even though there has been a growing awareness that the devastation caused by growth in such a short period of time is significant, irreversible, and universal and that we need to make a radical change, without being allowed to believe in the celebrated 'green growth.' Recently, there has been an accumulation of works denouncing the illusion of green growth and urging us to think radically, differently, to break with growth.

What are the conditions for a possible exit from growth, for a post-growth society? I would like to list them here. It seems to me that we need to adopt a new cosmology by refusing to accept the legacy of modernity and by questioning the Cartesian scheme of nature as an empty object reduced to an extension vis-à-vis a subject as thinker, master, and possessor. Philippe Descola (2013) has undoubtedly inflicted the great fourth wound on us Westerners by revealing that naturalism was only one type of ontology among others, that the way in which the modern West represented nature was the *least well-shared* thing on the planet, and that it was wrong to think that the separation between humans and non-humans corresponded to a more advanced stage in the evolution of humanity. We therefore need to reintegrate human societies into nature, to replace the paradigm of conquest and exploitation with a paradigm of care, to revise the all-too-human foundations of our disciplines, to demand this same reintegration, and to define a new *novum organum* that includes the human sciences within the limits of nature without becoming the servants of the natural sciences. For me, this is a prerequisite for any exit from our growth-intoxicated societies.

The second prerequisite is to adopt new wealth indicators that will somehow encapsulate and integrate our national accounting system in order to place our productive system within the limits defined by the two indicators that I mentioned above. The third prerequisite is to immediately engage in a policy of massive reduction of inequalities so that all those who today do not have access to the minimum amenities to live decently can benefit from a process that requires an investment by all. If I were to add that an extremely substantial additional public investment will be needed for at least 20 years to decarbonize our economy, I will have mentioned most of the actions that we should put in place, at least in the richest countries, in order to initiate what I call the *ecological conversion* of our societies.

What is still missing is a narrative that explains the benefits that we will be able to derive from such a process. In addition to reducing the risks caused by climate change and the loss of biodiversity, these benefits would range from regaining breathable air, reducing cancers and other sources of death caused by pollution, to finding useful and probably less taxing jobs. The latter will involve reviewing our organization of labor, whether it be the long and absurd global value chains or the way we organize power in companies. All of these elements should accompany this radical change toward an ecological society. We need such a narrative to generate the enthusiasm we will absolutely have to have, as resistance will be strong since vested interests will be upset and changes in our practices will be far-reaching.

Among these changes, which appear to be both causes and consequences of this process, I would like to spend a moment discussing the democratization of the economy and companies. Many authors, including Thomas Coutrot (see also his contribution in this volume), have emphasized the close links between alienation from work and refraining from voting in elections or voting for the extremes. This is why my colleagues Isabelle Ferreras, Julie Battilana, and I launched a manifesto for the democratization and decommodification of work in May 2020, at the end of the first pandemic-related confinement during which so many often low-status workers had demonstrated their immense usefulness, in the form of a declaration signed by 6000 researchers around the world and published in more than 40 national newspapers (see Ferreras/Battilana/Méda 2020; Fraser et al. 2020). In what later became the book *Le Manifeste travail: Démocratiser, démarchandiser, dépolluer* ("The Working Manifesto: Democratize, Decommodify, Decarbonize"; Ferreras/Battilana/Méda [eds.] 2020), we argue that it is high time to give labor investors the same rights and power as capital providers and propose that from now on workers' representatives should have as many votes as shareholders and that the main decisions of the company should be taken by an absolute majority of the whole, so that each party has a veto right.

Democratizing our companies is not only a direct consequence of the absolute centrality of workers in the functioning of society but also one of the best ways to set our societies on the path of ecological conversion. This is because workers are in the best position to know which new jobs they will be able to take up, how the inevitable changes in the workforce should be best carried out, and which mechanisms need to be put in place to decommodify work, avoid unemployment, and allow workers in the shrinking sectors to join the new sectors and the new jobs to be created as quickly and efficiently as possible.

Democratizing work and the economy and decommodifying labor thus appear to be central elements of an ecological transformation that will obviously require new coalitions. Just as in the 19th century, as Henri Hatzfeld has shown, it took the combined efforts of the labor movement, political leaders, physicians, and humanist employers to improve labor conditions, so too, in order to succeed in this process, will we need the simultaneous mobilization of young and not-so-young people, workers from all sectors, trade union leaders, employers who have understood that change must take place as quickly as possible, NGOs, political leaders, and scientists—a coalition of all who are willing to pursue a common cause, the urgency of which is growing every day.

Literature

Descola, Philippe (2013): Beyond Nature and Culture, Chicago: University of Chicago Press.

Ferreras, Isabelle/Battilana, Julie/Méda, Dominique (2020): "Let's democratize and decommodify work: Employees are the core constituency of the firm, but are mostly excluded from participating in the government of their workplaces—a right monopolized by capital investors," in: The Boston Globe. Available from: https://www.bostonglobe.com/2020/05/15/opinion/lets-democratize-decommodify-work/ [accessed 8/15/2021].

Ferreras, Isabelle/Battilana, Julie/Méda, Dominique (eds.) (2020): Le Manifeste travail: Démocratiser, démarchandiser, dépolluer, Montrouge: Seuil.

Fourquet, François (1980): Les Comptes de la puissance: Histoire de la comptabilité nationale et du Plan, Paris: Recherches.

Fraser, Nancy et al. (2020): "Humans are not resources: Coronavirus shows why we must democratise work," in: The Guardian. Available from: https://www.theguardian.com/commentisfree/2020/may/15/humans-resources-coronavirus-democratise-work-health-lives-market [accessed 8/15/2021].

Jany-Catrice, Florence/Marlier, Grégory (2020): La santé sociale des nouvelles régions françaises (2008–2016). Available from: https:

//halshs.archives-ouvertes.fr/halshs-02967607/document [accessed 8/15/2021].

Kuznets, Simon (1941): National Income and Its Composition, 1919–1938, Vol. 1, assisted by Lillian Epstein and Elizabeth Jenks, New York: National Bureau of Economic Research.

Méda, Dominique (1999): Qu'est-ce que la richesse? Paris: Aubier.

Money Creation as a Foundational Tool for Convivialism

Christian Arnsperger, Solène Morvant-Roux, Jean-Michel Servet, André Tiran

In the face of our current uncertainties, it seems relatively straightforward to reach a broad consensus around new ways of life, new consumption habits, new patterns of mobility, and new ways of learning as well as connecting with others and our environment. But what are the best means of attaining the convivial world of tomorrow?

When it comes to this question, one area that is all too rarely investigated concerns money. And yet, a while back, André Gorz (2005) emphasized that if, for instance, the financing of a universal basic income were to stimulate genuine social transformation, it would necessarily have to rely on a specific mechanism of money creation (also: Fourel 2019). He was right to link his ecological and political thinking to a broader reflection on the monetary model. We, too, intend to locate our discussion within this perspective (Arnsperger 2015).

Just as Pierre-Joseph Proudhon, a long time ago, had laid out the theoretical foundations upon which to build solidaristic and cooperative practices in finance, it appears to us that today an equally relevant change of paradigm is being offered by *Modern Money Theory*, or MMT for short (Wray 2015; Mitchell/Wray/Watts 2019). It constitutes the main alternative to the still very widespread misconception that debt or taxes *finance* public spending. By fundamentally uprooting conventional ideas about taxation and public debt, MMT stands as one of the most promising currents capable of providing a solid macroeconomic grounding for convivialism and its bottom-up change processes.

1. Leaving behind Conventional Ideas

Amid the current social and ecological crisis, it is becoming increasingly impossible on structural grounds to use tax revenues to cover expenses for income support and sensibly reorienting economic activities. This has led to a renewed focus on public *deficits* and *indebtedness* both on the left and on the right.

Financialized public debt—that is, debt that is transformed into government bonds traded on financial markets—is not merely a neutral source of fresh cash. According to conventional economic thought, it must inevitably lead, to a number of *austerity* measures. Such measures entail considerable political risks: Are we not once more going to witness drastic cuts in expenditures on healthcare, education, and ecological transition in the name of an orthodox conception that hardly anyone bothers to question? If these are the conditions, are convivialist hopes not bound to slowly wither away at the margins of society?

Does this mean public debt should be canceled? There are some who advance not only anthropological and ethical but also economic arguments in this direction (e.g., Graeber 2011; Toussaint/Saurin 2017). Given how low interest rates are currently, and are likely to remain, these bonds will yield almost nothing anyway. Others, by contrast, assert that while defaulting on their national debt may provide short-term relief to the states in question, in the longer run it represents a shortfall for which they will have to pay in one form or another because the financial markets will lose confidence.

However, as MMT underscores, this argument in fact rests on a crucial difference between the countries that possess monetary sovereignty and the ones that do not. It is only the latter who truly run the risk of witnessing their financialized debt being devalued by virtue of the alleged 'wisdom of the markets.' According to MMT, if the country monetizing its national debt instead of financializing it has monetary sovereignty, as in the case of the United States, the United Kingdom, Japan, or Switzerland, the market argument loses its clout. The notion of monetary sovereignty is therefore paramount for those who seek convivialist alternatives and feel the need to question the validity of the "myths" that surround public deficits and debt (Kelton 2020).

2. Sovereignty as a Key to the Debate

According to MMT, monetary sovereignty corresponds to five traits that define the latitude enjoyed by a government. (1) The latter chooses a unit of account in which its currency is denominated; (2) it imposes obligations (particularly in terms of taxes) denominated in that unit of account; (3) it is itself the issuer of the currency denominated in this unit of account and accepts this currency as payment for the imposed obligations; (4) if it issues other obligations against itself, they are likewise denominated in this unit of account and redeemable with the currency issued by the government; and (5) the exchange rate of this currency is floating, with the possibility for its central bank to purchase or sell foreign currency according to its needs (Wray 2020: 9 f.).

This has implications that go very much against the grain of conventional economic thought: A sovereign currency issuer never faces a "budget constraint," can never "run out of money," is always able to fulfill its own obligations (including any interest payments on its own government bonds) in its own currency, and has the ability to fix the interest rate for any of the bonds it issues (ibid.: 10).

Once one adopts the analytical lens of MMT, the absence or loss of monetary sovereignty turns out to be part of the injustice a country is suffering—a contingent historical construct born out of power relations—rather than merely being part of its timeless features; it is condemned to a kind of powerlessness. For a country with monetary sovereignty, the question, *How much will it cost?* is secondary compared to the question, *Through what social and environmental policy measures can we make our society more livable, more convivial, more humane?* MMT does not solve or silence debates about values; it merely finally frees them from the shackles imposed by the absence of monetary sovereignty.

Governments with monetary sovereignty do not need prior tax revenues in order to *finance* their expenditures. By making expenditures—which are generated simply via accounting entries by the central bank in favor of the treasury on the basis of budgets voted by parliament—that exceed their tax revenues, these governments are effectively making *net injections of currency* into the economy, which have positive effects as long as they do not generate inflation, do not cause the exchange rate to collapse, and do not lead to an overstepping of the planet's ecological boundaries.

In this context, to speak of a public *deficit*—in other words, a shortfall that would need to be 'made up for' through higher future revenues or lower future expenditures—is to pretend that a state with monetary sovereignty should think and operate like a household, business, region, canton, or like a state that (such as France in 1999 or Greece in 2001) has divested itself of its monetary sovereignty.

In reality, it is not pre-existing tax revenues that generate public expenditure. Rather, it is precisely the reverse: It is public expenditure that, once brought into circulation, makes it possible to generate additional economic activity and revenues, which in turn generate the possibility and the obligation to pay taxes. A state with monetary sovereignty does not go into deficit through its expenditures any more than we would say a bank goes into deficit by extending loans. And contrary to a bank, which in principle is not permitted to incur excessive loan-default risks, a currency-issuing government cannot go bankrupt.

If we are to ever truly imagine a future along convivialist lines, we need to start getting used to this new way of thinking and to demand that our decision-makers do so as well.

3. Public Deficits and Inflation

Conventional economic thinking criticizes MMT for condoning unbridled public expenditure, abandoning all fiscal prudence, and ultimately undermining confidence in the currency itself because of inflation. Who is right?

Government expenditures financed by public money creation flow into the hands of a host of actors—in this case, the beneficiaries of public entitlements and benefits and, subsequently, all those with whom they are connected. In this way, when the recipients of a universal basic income spend it on food, it is the providers of food who will receive it and then pass it along to their own suppliers, employees, landlords, and so on, with part of it even returning to the government in the form of various taxes.

MMT does not rule out that there might be situations where this public money creation generates inflation. It all depends on the macroeconomic context and on how close the economy is to *overheating*. Historically, hyperinflation is in general the consequence of a massive collapse of production, which creates sudden, large excess demand. The increase in currency issuance is only one of the symptoms and very rarely the cause (Alt 2020: 68–72). In the case of a transition towards conviviality, substantial public means will need to be devoted to financing forms of enterprise, ways of life, and public policies that generate new infrastructures, new kinds of jobs, and new ways of producing and consuming, along with the emergence of a new relationship to nature. There is nothing in these measures that ominously foreshadows a sudden, large excess demand.

MMT makes it possible to focus on the issues that really count. First of all, we constantly need to remind ourselves that the *deficits* and *debt* of a state with monetary sovereignty are a net injection of monetary means that can be mobilized by the people for their projects. Second, we need to ask ourselves above what threshold(s) the expenditures of a sovereign government via public money creation will become inflationary and also socially and ecologically detrimental, which requires us to inquire about the *quality*, the *nature*, and the *destination* of expenditures and not just their amount. And third, we need to realize that reflecting on a convivialist future in the context of monetary sovereignty has very little in common with reflecting on it in a context where this monetary sovereignty does not exist, has been lost, or has been given up.

Is not the risk here one of fetishizing the state while neglecting bottom-up social connections and the logic of the commons? This is certainly an important question, but it does not imply that we should, in return, carelessly neglect the social and ecological benefits of public money creation when it is non-inflationary.

4. Inequality, Jobs, and Ecological Footprint

Focusing ideologically on financial debt is wrong because it sidelines—and even makes invisible—the "deficits that really count" (Kelton 2020: chap. 7): that is, the accumulation of ecological debt due to the fact that the human footprint grows ever heavier owing to the currently prevailing orientation of both bank loans and public expenditures as well as the insufficient availability of such essential public goods as education, health, social security, and the possibility of exercising a socially useful activity.

This is where MMT resonates most directly with the perspectives opened up by convivialism. The public funding of autonomous activities as well as of a wide range of social, cultural, and ecological experimentation clearly forms part of any future *good society*.

One of MMT's main contributions to the debate around social policy is its proposal of a *permanent and unconditional public employment guarantee*, financed through public money creation (e.g., Tcherneva 2020). The idea is that the government offers each unemployed citizen the possibility (but does not impose the obligation) of getting a public-sector job with a good wage and full social benefits. This proposal cannot, of course, be seen as a panacea for all the complex issues linked to unemployment and underemployment (Giraud 2015), nor does it render unemployment insurance unnecessary. However, it does fit into the spirit of what convivialism intends to offer in the future, albeit in a somewhat different form compared to what MMT itself is advocating. We are thinking here, in particular, of a generalization of Sophie Swaton's (2018; 2020) idea of an "ecological transition income," the logic of which could be emulated by combining two elements: on the one hand, national or federal public money creation; on the other, decentralization in the use of the funds thus generated, via local-level associations or cooperatives tasked with selecting economic projects that produce high social and/or ecological "value-added." The projects could, for example, be required to obey a set of principles that derive from the Social and Solidarity Economy (SSE). They could also be asked to cohere with the logic of Kate Raworth's "doughnut" (2017), according to which each project has to demonstrate that its activities do not overstep planetary boundaries.

Ultimately, what is called for within a convivialist approach is the close merging of MMT with the approach of "permacircularity" set out by Arnsperger/Bourg (2017; also Arnsperger 2021). We need to realize that our financial, relational, cultural, social, and ecological deficits all interact, and we have to invert their currently prevailing hierarchy. Money creation needs to be put at the service of the economy, which has to serve society and culture, which in turn need to be recognized as integral parts of the biosphere. At the end of the day, the positive synergy between convivialism, permacircularity, and MMT could finally make it possible to fully implement a notion of *strong sustainability*—a notion that is sorely missing from the great majority of current debates on ecological transition or the need for an ecological revolution.

It is clear, for instance, that currently ongoing discussions about a Green New Deal are still much too closely framed by a notion of weak sustainability, especially when held up against the options of convivialism, which are much closer to the thought of André Gorz and Ivan Illich. And yet, the straightjacket of the discourse on budget constraints and deficit reduction is an even more powerful conversation stopper. Taking into account the advantages of monetary sovereignty can definitely liberate debates and experimental energies.

5. A Fetishization of the State?

From the point of view of convivialism, the danger of some of MMT's propositions lies in a *statist* vision of society, carrying with it a conception of money that might well be too unilaterally public and neglects its common-good dimensions. Up to what point is it acceptable for the state to be the dominant actor when it comes to supporting convivialism through re-framed rules of money creation?

Indeed, unless one is tempted to indulge in a certain form of fetishization of the central government, one simply has to acknowledge that money is not just a creature of the state. It is a commons, linked neither exclusively to the sphere of the market nor exclusively to the sphere of the state but also to the logic of sharing and reciprocity. It is therefore crucial to be able to think about the conditions for currency issuance for private-sector purposes other than by swinging back in simplistic fashion from public money creation towards bank-money creation.

What emerges as a third way, both compatible with certain core intuitions of MMT and more in tune with convivialism and its advocacy of the commons, is the idea of *monetary pluralism* (Lietaer et al. 2018; also: Blanc 2018).

6. Money as a Public Good and as a Commons

MMT neglects monetary pluralism's *commons* dimension of currency emission and fails to recognize the importance—which convivialist circles, among others, have emphasized—of creating and managing currencies locally (Fourel 2017). Yet if, for instance, a version of MMT's public employment guarantee in the form of an "ecological transition income" is to revive and enliven local economies, it might be sensible to pay out certain portions of wages in local complementary currencies. It is therefore necessary to combine the reforms proposed by MMT with other monetary experiments that have emerged at the local level. Aside from local complementary currencies, this necessity can be illustrated through experiments such as local exchange trading systems (LETS) as well as territorially anchored fiscal currencies (such as the Argentinian *bonos* in 2000 or the Californian IOUs in 2008). To varying degrees, their management relies on collaboration between stakeholders, which helps promote new forms of deliberative democracy and re-politicize the debates around money.

This is not in opposition to MMT, however. What we need is to rethink the complementarity between instruments at different scales. This provides a basis for enriching MMT even if it means introducing concepts and tools that seem foreign to it at first glance.

One of the advantages of combining MMT with plural/grassroots money creation that is neither state- nor bank-driven is that many governments devoid of monetary sovereignty in the strict sense, or having voluntarily given it up, could open a channel that would allow them to recover *from the bottom up* a certain kind of monetary *sovereignty*.

Take, for instance, the case of a eurozone country such as France. The question is the following: What would be preferable? A total absence of monetary sovereignty that makes it arduous to implement any of the socioecological reforms discussed in this article? Or the deliberate acceptance and even encouragement of a plurality of non-state, non-bank currencies: between businesses, such as the Swiss WIR; within local communities, such as LETS and other mutual-credit currencies; within towns or regions, in the form of regional complementary currencies? In neither case will the French government revert to actually being monetarily sovereign once again. But while in the first case it remains subject to a single, supranational currency that coerces it into passivity through the tyranny of an outdated paradigm of *monetary correctness*, in the second case it allows its citizens to exercise an admittedly restricted but nevertheless tangible sovereignty.

In our eyes, the answer is clear. Faced with the urgency of exiting the current crises by convivialist means and of transitioning towards strong sustainability, a government must either attempt to fully recover its monetary sovereignty by reverting to being an issuer of its own national currency, in which case it can start directly benefiting from the insights provided by MMT; or it must encourage monetary pluralization within its borders, thus at least endowing itself, from the bottom up, with part of the sovereignty that it never had or that it lost.

Literature

Alt, John D. (2020): Paying Ourselves to Save the Planet: A Layman's Explanation of Modern Money Theory, independently published.

Arnsperger, Christian (2015): "Revenu de base, économie soutenable et alternatives monétaires," in: L'Économie politique 67, pp. 34–49.

Arnsperger, Christian (2021): Permacircular Horizons. Available from: https://arnsperger-perma-circular.com/ [accessed 8/15/2021].

Arnsperger, Christian/Bourg, Dominique (2017): Écologie intégrale: Pour une société permacirculaire, Paris: Presses Universitaires de France.

Blanc, Jérôme (2018): Les monnaies alternatives, Paris: La Découverte.

Fourel, Christophe (2017): "Le convivialisme et les monnaies complémentaires," in: Humbert, Marc (ed.), Reconstruction de la société: Analyses convivialistes, Rennes: Presses Universitaires de Rennes, pp. 95–102.

Fourel, Christophe (2019): "Sortie du capitalisme, revenu d'existence et monnaies alternatives dans la pensée de Gorz," in: Variations 22. Available from: https://doi.org/10.4000/variations.1194 [accessed 8/15/ 2021].

Giraud, Pierre-Noël (2015): L'Homme inutile: Du bon usage de l'économie, Paris: Odile Jacob.

Gorz, André (2005): "Richesse sans valeur, valeur sans richesse: Interview with Sonia Montaño," in: Cadernos IHV Ideias 31. Available from: https://inventin.lautre.net/livres/Gorz-Richesse-sans-valeur.pdf [accessed 8/15/2021].

Graeber, David (2011): Debt: The First 5,000 Years, Brooklyn: Melville House.

Kelton, Stephanie (2020): The Deficit Myth: Modern Monetary Theory and How to Build a Better Economy, London: John Murray.

Lietaer, Bernard/Arnsperger, Christian/Brunnhuber, Stefan/Goerner, Sally (2012): Money and Sustainability: The Missing Link, Charmouth: Triarchy Press.

Mitchell, William/Wray, L. Randall/Watts, Martin (2019): Macroeconomics, London: Red Globe Press.

Raworth, Kate (2017): Doughnut Economics: Seven Ways to Think Like a 21st-Century Economist, White River Junction: Chelsea Green.

Swaton, Sophie (2018): Pour un revenu de transition écologique, Paris: Presses Universitaires de France.

Swaton, Sophie (2020): Revenu de transition écologique: Mode d'emploi, Paris: Presses Universitaires de France.

Tcherneva, Pavlina (2020): The Case for a Job Guarantee, Cambridge, UK: Polity Press.

Toussaint, Éric/Saurin, Patrick (2017): Le système dette: Histoire des dettes souveraines et de leur répudiation, Paris: Les Liens qui Libèrent.

Wray, L. Randall (2015): Modern Money Theory: A Primer on Macroeconomics for Sovereign Monetary Systems, 2nd ed., New York: Palgrave Macmillan.

Wray, L. Randall (2020): "Alternative Paths to Modern Monetary Theory," in: Edward Fullbrook/Jamie Morgan (eds.): Modern Monetary Theory and Its Critics, Bristol: World Economics Association Books, pp. 8–46.

Pluriversalism and Nature

Conviviality to Reanimate the World

Geneviève Azam

Is it possible to imagine a convivial world for tomorrow? One that springs to mind is *Ecotopia*, a "semi-utopian" novel by Ernest Callenbach, published in 1975. Brice Matthieussent (2018 [1975]: 11; my translation), who wrote the preface for the French edition, states that it is not "the fictional description of a perfect world but of a perfectible world that would nevertheless be on the right track." Its story illustrates a concrete and desirable path that began with the secession of three western American states—California, Oregon, and Washington—and their reunion in Ecotopia. It is an inspiring fiction, both a manifesto and a cry of warning. Instead of an accomplished convivial world, perhaps we should imagine a convivial path?

Taking this route diverts us from the initial question. If the future is largely unpredictable, it is certain that the world will not be convivial if, in seeking tomorrow, we go beyond present worlds and follow the temptation to state abstract, ideal principles, oblivious in their projection to both the dangers and the potentialities of the present. If convivialism is a political art for living together, for shaping the world, then it is a lucid experience of this present, a resistance, a test, so much so that our concrete experiences bear the stigmata of the end of worlds, of plunder, of the destruction of living environments, of the reign of force and injustice, of capitalist chaos. The terrifying accounts in the autumn of 2020 that came out of Oregon in the United States, mixing pandemic, enormous fires, extreme right-wing militias patrolling the streets of Portland, and racist crimes, were approaching apocalyptic dystopias (Raymond 2020). They have demonstrated what is at stake.

Conviviality is also a daily challenge in the wake of the concrete effects of the terrifying utopia, dressed up in the robes of freedom, called "neo-liberal," which is producing humans who are increasingly atomized, precarious, lonely and massified, controlled, detached from earthly ties and dependent on a sprawling megamachine that is accelerating the war on life. If "convivial" means "a modern society of responsibly limited tools," as Ivan Illich (1975 [1973]: 12) wrote, it might seem inaccessible at a time when technical and industrial infrastructures have crossed thresholds that confine the Earth, bodies, and minds in a universe that deprives us of our ability to breathe, our sensations, and our autonomy. The convivial approach is then contained in the art of blocking, diverting, dismantling, abandoning, and inventing new convivial tools, both technical and institutional ones. In France, the success of the cooperative *L'atelier paysan*, which designs tools that are compatible with agro-ecology instead of equipment for war against the land, is one example among many others.

By determinedly walking this thorny path, lest we give in to the *hubris* that conviviality would like to avoid, we do not encounter the world in the singular but rather single and entangled worlds. Alongside the deafening world of the winners, there are sleepwalking and silent worlds; and also worlds that have disappeared, become mutilated, abandoned, rendered invisible, or are in the process of collapse; and finally, other worlds that emerge from dissident and resistant communities committed to living together in the environments of life, to taking care of humans and the Earth. To walk this path is to experience vulnerability, to go to the extremes of this experience, not to overcome it but to cultivate the hope of an awakening and of new solidarities.

Convivialism is also a way of meeting worlds that are confronted with the Western tradition, as is the case with many indigenous peoples who survived the loss of their world several centuries ago. A convivial approach takes their cosmologies, thoughts, and practices seriously, opening up toward and allowing oneself to be decentered and destabilized by other points of view and restoring a relationship to the world and to the Earth that is more complex and subtle than the dominant reductionism. This is the approach of "Amazonian perspectivism" analyzed by Viveiros de Castro (1998). Conviviality is thus no longer just an ethic and a politics of human relationships. It extends to other existing terrestrial beings in order to share a world. It is a strategy for survival.

If there is a crucial decentering, it is precisely that of anthropocentrism and of the great separation between nature and culture, mind and body, which is at the heart of Western culture. The detachment from the Earth, from its communities of living beings, excludes any conviviality between humans and non-humans. And it authorizes the separation between humans themselves. In the same way, it denies the spiritual part of nature and the natural part of humans. Seeking to climb to the top of the evolutionary ladder, as sovereign subjects and the ultimate species, with the promise of human perfection and exceptionalism reduces us to simplified, lonely human beings, entirely proprietors of ourselves and of the world, exiled from our earthly condition, from our living environments, deprived of relations with the thousands of organisms that weave the web of life and with the natural entities that shelter us and threaten us as we ignore and destroy them. The last step on this ladder is toward the trans-human; the others have failed, and before we destroy ourselves, we should leave the ladder and accept our vulnerability among the living.

The Earth, the source of life, has become a globe, a narrow, external totality, a resource at the service of human *well-being*. Colonialism, capitalism, and industrialism have been able to nourish themselves on it and organize the unlimited extraction of the wealth that it makes available. This naturalist ontology, in the words of Philippe Descola, is recent and singular in the history of humanity. After the Renaissance, writes historian and ecofeminist philosopher Carolyn Merchant (1990: 68), "a slow but unidirectional alienation from the immediate daily organic relationship that had formed the basis of human experience from the earliest times was occurring." It has allowed the naturalization of a section of humanity—the uncivilized, the barbaric, the female—and has justified colonial domination and patriarchy. It has ignored the web of life, the multiple interdependencies that constitute us. Philosopher Glenn Albrecht (2019) recalls, not without mischief, the early contribution in this field of women biologists, often marginalized, Elyne Mitchell, Lynn Margulis, or Rachel Carson and her seminal book *Silent Spring* (1962).

A convivial world would seek to re-establish these links to dethrone human, virilist arrogance. Experiences of vulnerability on an unprecedented scale, as well as scientific work showing the role of cooperation, altruism, and conviviality in evolution, instead of domination, competition, and force, should facilitate this task. Not to mention the research in evolutionary biology that attests to the complex cognitive forms in other living beings. Life is not a struggle of competing autonomous entities. Human exceptionalism and separation, which are the hallmarks of rationality, have shriveled reason and plunged us into darkness—to the point of threatening the continuation of life.

The Australian ecofeminist philosopher Val Plumwood, who since the 1970s has exposed the dead-end of the belief in the discontinuity between humans and other-than-humans, made her encounter with a saltwater crocodile the philosophical experience of such a decentering. "Being food for other animals shakes our image of human mastery. As eaters of others who can never ourselves be eaten in turn by them or even conceive of ourselves in edible terms, we take, but do not give" (Plumwood 2012: 19). This is another way of thinking about the ecological catastrophe as a breakdown in the system of giving and the triple obligation of *giving–receiving–giving back*, which, in the face of a de-animated nature, an inert matter, would make no sense.

To rediscover an animated nature is also to regain its vital capacity and our own ungovernable part in a time when it is actually under threat. Thus, Plumwood invites us to seriously devise an intentional strategy for other-than-humans in order to *negotiate* our membership in an ecological community. She calls for a philosophical, non-doctrinaire animism that is embodied in a way of living, a poetics of existence, an attentive presence driven by the gratitude for experiencing ourselves as alive. This materialist animism intersects with the work of ethologists who confirm the intelligence of natural entities and their intentionality: They are neither mindless things nor machines responding to stimuli. Animism in the "developed" world is often brandished like a scarecrow, whereas "humanity is [actually] universally and phenomenologically animistic," write Alain Caillé, Philippe Chanial, and Fabrice Flipo (2013: 15; my translation). This rejection is nourished by a notion of animism defined in the colonial tradition and in the terms of dualism by the belief in the presence of humanoid spirits in inanimate matter. It was the basis of the criminal split between "us," the rational civilized, and "them," the obscurantist animists. The world could be enlightened again by the spirit of things, places, and living beings on Earth, and by life as a convivial relationship with others.

Thus, if conviviality, in the wake of Ivan Illich (1975 [1973]: 64), supposes to dismantle the world as a "technological totality," it is also the mechanistic vision of nature that needs to be undermined. The path that Illich opened toward a radical ecology must still be explored. Defining the convivial society as a new way "to articulate the triadic relationship between persons, tools, and a new collectivity" (ibid.: 12), his ecological thinking focuses on the limits of the Earth in relation to the globality of the hyper-industrialized world that was taking shape half a century before he published *Tools for Conviviality*. This was the major and unacknowledged issue of that era, which was all about endless growth and development and which triggered the chaos of the present world by exceeding these limits. Our present age, faced with the dangers of life extinction and climate chaos, demands a new look at nature, not only in its limits to industrial excess but in its potentialities: "It's a matter of being *open to experiences of nature as powerful, agentic and creative, making space in our culture for an animating sensibility and vocabulary*" (Plumwood 2009: 126). If it is indeed a question of humans freeing themselves from the prison of overpowered machines, 'welfare bureaucrats,' and tools that disrupt the balance between man and nature, this balance requires a decentering. This would enable us to discover ourselves as empathic beings and bodies attached to an ecological web and to be sensitive again to limits, dependencies, and entanglements with other-than-human worlds. Perhaps in this way we can learn all the valuable lessons from the current pandemic and other disasters.

Being attentive to the worlds and voices of others is a way of regaining control of our destiny in order to avoid a fatal end to the present catastrophes. Cultivating our attachments gives substance to concrete utopias, to our ways of cultivating, inhabiting, commuting, working, and sharing. It is a commitment to the beauty of the world. On January 1, 2021, the Zapatistas published *A Declaration.... for Life*, which has already been signed by hundreds of groups around the world (EZLN 2021). They will visit all five continents to share it. Let us welcome them.

Literature

Albrecht, Glenn A. (2019): Earth Emotions: New Words for a New World, Ithaca: Cornell University Press.

Caillé, Alain/Chanial, Philippe/Flipo, Fabrice (2012): "Présentation," in: Revue du MAUSS 42, pp. 5–23. Available from: https://www.cairn.info/revue-du-mauss-2013-2.htm [accessed 8/15/2021].

Callenbach, Ernest (1975): Ecotopia: The Notebooks and Reports of William Weston, Berkley, CA: Banyan Tree Books.

l'EZLN (2021): "Pour la vie: Les Zapatistes Visiteront les 5 continents" – Première Partie: Une Déclaration... pour la vie. Available from: http://www.csia-nitassinan.org/spip.php?article1171 [accessed 8/15/2021].

Illich, Ivan (1975 [1973]): Tools for Conviviality, New York: Fontana/Collins.

Matthieussent, Brice (2018 [1975]): "Changer: Préface," in: Ernest Callenbach: Écotopia: Notes personnelles et articles de William Weston, Paris: Rue de l'échiquier, pp. 11–15.

Merchant, Carolyn (1990): The Death of Nature: Women, Ecology, and the Scientific Revolution, San Francisco: HarperCollins.

Plumwood, Val (2009): "Nature in the Active Voice," in: Australian Humanities Review 46, pp. 113–129.

Plumwood, Val (2012): The Eye of the Crocodile, ed. by Lorraine Shannon, Canberra: Australian National University E Press.

Raymond, Jon (2020): "Tribune – Culture et idées: L'année où nous avons suffoqué," in: Reporterre. Available from: https://reporterre.net/L-annee-ou-nous-avons-suffoque?utm_source=newsletter&utm_medium=email&utm_campaign=nl_hebdo [accessed 8/15/2021].

Viveiros de Castro, Eduardo (1998): "Cosmological Deixis and Amerindian Perspectivism," in: The Journal of the Royal Anthropological Institute 4, pp. 469–488.

Convivial Conservation with Nurturing Masculinities in Brazil's Atlantic Forest

Susan Paulson, Jonathan DeVore, Eric Hirsch

This chapter explores convivial conservation, an emerging paradigm that supports care and interdependence among human and other life toward purposes of mutual regeneration and thriving. Rather than defending endangered nature from destructive people, this approach fosters intertwined human-environment care, wellbeing, and justice on multiple scales.

During decades of ethnographic research in South America, we coauthors have witnessed and reflected on practices and conditions that variously support or constrain convivial conservation. The following scenes from our learning experiences offer glimpses into life-worlds that enrich horizons of possibility for other kinds of populations who face the challenge of developing ways to live together with meaning and joy, while reducing the degrading exploitation of humans and other nature.

One September afternoon in 2014 in the Colca Valley of Peru's southern Andes, where Hirsch conducted two years of ethnographic research, he filmed three farmers singing to their land after a satisfying day of collaborative labor. The bass-toned voices of Dons Máximo, Sabino, and Gerardo reverberated down multiple terraces into the valley below, beseeching the earth to allow the seeds they had just planted to be warm and to bear fruit. Before singing, they had hydrated themselves and the terrain with *chicha*, a drink of fermented maize and barley that marks rituals and celebrations. In a chant called *Hialeo*, their Quechua-language verses shouted out the name of the feminine-gendered terrain,

"Mama Ch'ela," and praised the *Pachamama*, the oxen who pulled their plows, their planting tools, their home villages, and their families. Ending the long day in convivial celebration, singing to and with the land and each other, and nourishing the land and each other with chicha, is a gratifying form of conserving and sustaining relationships of reciprocity among farmers, seeds, and soil.

One September morning in 2002 in rural Bahia, Brazil, where DeVore and Paulson conducted research over many years, DeVore joined a group of men clearing the young rainforest that had regrown on an abandoned plantation called *Nossa Senhora*. As Colodino, his brothers, and their sons labored together, their calls and laughter reverberated through the forest, together with sounds of machetes, axes, and a borrowed chainsaw. Weeks after clearing understory vegetation, they would burn the plot; plant manioc, beans, and bananas; and eventually cultivate rich agroforests with perennial trees. This day of collaborative labor also culminated in convivial celebration, as participants played dominos, listened to *seresta* music, and shared a bottle of *cachaça*. Into the evening, impassioned conversations evolved around 'environmentalists' who condemn them for destroying the rainforest.

This chapter traces the emergence of vital interdependencies among human and other life in the second scenario, set in Brazil's highly biodiverse Atlantic Forest, which is home to a long history of struggles by indigenous peoples, enslaved Africans, and others seeking to forge alternatives to extractivist economies that degrade human and non-human life. We focus on a group of people who have built affirming lifeworlds on land they occupied in the 1990s. Such squatters are frequently condemned as threats to society and adversaries of nature. Yet, over the years, we have been repeatedly inspired by their commitments to care for each other and for more than human lives by nurturing native trees, nourishing wild birds, protecting water sources, and similar gestures.

Whereas indigenous people and rural women are often stereotyped as guardians of nature, the protagonists of this chapter are the kinds of men who tend to be characterized as destroyers. Their journeys toward nurturing experiences and expressions of masculinity illuminate the potential of (re)distributive politics to move men out of jobs that degrade their bodies and environments, and the potential of mutually sustaining interspecies relationships to build satisfying identities.

In this chapter, we seek to provoke reflections and debate about possibilities for forging futures with healthier gender roles and human-environment relations. Appreciation of convivialism in our research processes may motivate further methodological innovations. Our attention to conservation operating beyond formal nature preserves contributes to findings of surprisingly diverse intimacies among human and other lives (Haraway 2016; Hirsch 2017; Singh 2017). Finally, we celebrate the role of convivial conservation in restoring senses of joy, abundance, and festiveness through relations of solidarity.

1. Convivial Conservation

In heated debates about conservation, exclusionary approaches that use fences and guns to keep humans out of nature preserves are pitted against participatory projects that train local residents to manage preserves in approved ways (e.g., Agrawal/Redford 2009; Brockington/Duffy/Igoe 2008). Despite strong differences, both approaches reinforce the conceptual dichotomy, and practical segregation, of humanness from wilderness. The strategy of securing conservation by divorcing humans from other nature is exemplified in "Half-Earth" proposals, championed by E. O. Wilson (2016) and other scientists, who propose to designate 50 percent of the Earth's land mass and water area as a patchwork of conservation zones, protected from human life and economic activities. While some proposals allow extremely small roles for select groups such as rural women and indigenous residents, these approaches portend forced removal and resettlement of historically marginalized populations (Büscher et al. 2017). Visions of conservation through perpetual segregation militate against principles of *The Second Convivialist Manifesto* (Convivialist International 2020 [hereafter cited as: *SCM*]).

Convivial conservation, pioneered by Bram Büscher and Robert Fletcher (2020), is an integrated Whole Earth approach that responds to ecological, social, and political-economic forces and factors that are undermining biocultural diversity in the 21st century. It does not focus blame on marginalized people who perform destructive work that degrades their bodies and other nature, such as coal miners of West Virginia, gold miners of Brazil's Serra Pelada, or, in the case discussed here, laborers in monocrop plantations carved into tropical forest. Instead, by addressing and redressing structural relationships that undergird and compel this mutual violence, convivial conservation seeks to renew affirming interdependencies among human and other life.

While considering scenes from rural Brazil, we invite readers to ask: What roles can and do relations with non-human others play in the formation of good lives? How might conservation and care for diverse organisms and environments be bound up with conservation and care for human communities? We hope the case will motivate you to join our reflection on principles outlined in the *SCM* (7):

> "*Principle of common naturality*: Humans do not live outside a nature, of which they should become 'masters and possessors.' Like all living beings, they are part of it and are interdependent with it. They have a responsibility to take care of it. If they do not respect it, it is their ethical and physical survival that is at risk.
> *Principle of common humanity*: Beyond differences of skin, nationality, language, culture, religion, or wealth, sex, or gender, there exists only one humanity, which must be respected in the person of each of its members.
> *Principle of common sociality*: Human beings are social beings for whom the greatest wealth is the richness of the concrete relationships they maintain among themselves within associations, societies, or communities of varying size and nature."

2. Methods: From Collecting Data to Living and Learning With

Our understanding of this case developed over long-term engagements. Between 2001 and 2009, Paulson led field research schools in Bahia for six weeks each year. In addition to practicing scientific techniques for gathering information, participants were encouraged to learn by actively *living with* humans and other nature, including the settlement Nossa Senhora. DeVore participated as a student in one of these field schools, and subsequently completed 38 months of ethnographic and ethnohistorical research in the region between 2002 and 2012. Our understandings expressed here are also enriched by studies elsewhere in South America, including 13 years of research that Hirsch carried out with Quechua farmers in the Peruvian Andes, and 20 years of research that Paulson pursued in Bolivia.

All of us engage methods that might be called convivial, joining enthusiastically in long days of labor, celebrations, and relaxation, in which we not only observe, but also experience and connect with people and surroundings. We also experiment with more mutual and less hierarchical practices of knowledge production, exemplified by the video project described below, which fosters creative agency among local participants.

The three co-authors of this chapter shared and discussed our observations in several conferences and workshops, and subsequently co-authored the article, "Conserving human and other nature: A curious case of convivial conservation from Brazil" (DeVore/Hirsch/Paulson 2019). The present chapter develops from that longer article, which also explores the instrumentalization of indigeneity in conservation-related legislation, projects, and scholarship.

3. Historical Violence, Redistributive Justice, Convivial Conservation

Since European colonization, Brazil's highly biodiverse Atlantic Forest has been the site of conflict among competing interests including profit-driven extractivism and state-directed timber conservation (Dean 1995). During the first half of the 20th century, former slaves and other people squatted in the region's hills where they cultivated manioc gardens, foraged, fished, and hunted. Stories told by former members of these communities recall lives that emphasized sharing, reciprocity, and social reproduction (DeVore 2014). Beginning in the 1950s, however, this world was dismantled through a protracted land grab inaugurated by one of Brazil's most infamous capitalists, Norberto Odebrecht, who appropriated the region's timber resources and sold the land to investors, notably Firestone, seeking to plant rubber (DeVore 2018). As resident families were expelled, men and some women were repurposed as plantation laborers.

A new phase of struggles emerged in the early 1990s, when a *witch's broom* fungus (*Moniliophthora perniciosa*) devastated the region's commercial cacao plantations, prompting owners to abandon their land and causing workers to lose their wages. In the wake of this disaster, native vegetation regrew vigorously, and groups of former plantation workers, together with their families, occupied and began to cultivate plantation lands for themselves.

Especially in the early years, members of these nascent communities employed machetes, axes, and chainsaws, together with fire, to open spaces for cultivation. As they slashed-and-burned forest to create space for their own life-worlds, these squatters were condemned—like generations of swidden farmers around the world—as ignorant enemies of nature. One community member named Damião pointed out with irony how Brazil's environmental protection agency did so much to protect jaguars, but nothing to protect small farmers, protesting: "I have no interest in cutting down a tree. But I have to survive."

But Damião and others were not just felling trees. They were emancipating themselves by building meaningful and sustaining relationships with land, plants, animals, and other aspects of their biophysical world. Over the years, we witnessed burned forests transform into bountiful agroforests, producing foodstuffs like manioc, bananas, beans and vegetables, and cash crops such as cacao and rubber, under the shade of volunteer saplings (DeVore 2017).

4. Interspecies Care and Affection Express Common Naturality

Moved by the enthusiasm with which these Brazilian men express joy and affection for trees, and the Peruvian farmers described above sing loving gratitude to the soil, we explore various methods to learn about interspecies relationships. In 2009, one farmer asked DeVore to video record the interwoven stories of his life, his family, and their farm. The video became so popular that others asked DeVore to record their stories, too, resulting in the co-production of fourteen videos. Inspired by this method, Felipe Pinheiro, a graduate student working with Paulson, co-produced similar videos in 2019 with silvopastoralists in the Bacia do Jacuípe region of Bahia (Canal Agroecologia 2020).

In July 2010, DeVore collaborated with Floriano to record his family's story, which highlighted mutual care and provisioning with plants and animals. Pointing to various crops that his family cultivated, such as the fruit-producing *cupuaçu* tree (*Theobroma grandiflorum*), Floriano explained, "It's good to plant plenty of fruit [...] the fruit will reveal itself, it'll say: '*I'm here*.' It's like the cupuaçu saying, '*I'm here. We've arrived at the time for me to give to you.*'"

Since his family began to occupy and cultivate their corner of Nossa Senhora, Floriano has planted seeds and seedlings, including *pequi* and *aderno* trees, numerous *sucupira* trees, and two dozen *jatobá* trees. In the following quote, he remembers planting half a dozen *oti* trees on his birthday twelve years earlier:

"Passing through neighboring forests, I saw some good *oti* seedlings there, I brought them to see if they'd take root, if they'd grow. I planted this *oti* tree here. The thing suffered, but he began to extend himself, saying, '*I'll rise, I'll rise.*' [...] They say that for him to give fruit, it takes 30 years. I say, '*I wanna see.*' It was planted one day, it was my birthday. On my birthday I went there, planted him."

Deep temporal horizons are revealed by Floriano's motivations to cultivate trees that are elsewhere valued for their hardwood timber, a resource that Floriano would not live to harvest:

"I plant because nature asks for it. The land asks for plants. So, if the land asks, and there are no trees here, the farmer has to bring them from elsewhere to plant. That's why I plant. [...] And this example that I'm making here, I want it to serve for a century. So that all who may come work the earth, who have their little farm, and also plant three or four or five trees, to show their children and to show their grandchildren and great-grandchildren."

These words from rural Brazil evoke lines from Wendell Berry, the Kentucky poet-farmer who, in a well-loved poem "Manifesto: The Mad Farmer Liberation Front," writes:

"Invest in the millennium. Plant sequoias.
Say that your main crop is the forest
that you did not plant,
that you will not live to harvest."

Floriano recalled that some companions jokingly asked him: "What'll you do with those trees, eat them?" To which he replied: "I don't eat it. But the birds eat, the others [...]. As long as they go there, they don't come to eat off my plate [...]. If I don't plant for them, they'll come eat off my plate." "This year," he observed, the aderno trees "put out plenty of fruit. I've got plenty of seeds here on the ground [...] this is food for birds, toucans, *inguaxo* [*Cacicus haemorrhous*], and even the *paca* [*Cuniculus paca*]." He explained that if he did not plant something for the animals and insects, they would go directly to his cacao: "Cacao is the food that we [humans] want most, so we'll share with them [...]. We give—we plant for them, too."

In conventional economic terms, Floriano's orientation to the trees that he cultivates is non-utilitarian: they offer nothing for his family to eat or sell. Environmental impact assessments may illuminate the trees' contributions to ecosystems services or agroforestry, yet fail to capture the wholeness of interspecies commitment. Floriano's insistence on planting for nature and for future generations, and planting so that insects, birds, and mammals can also eat, represents an interesting convergence with arguments for Half-Earth-style conservation. Both perceive that the ability to provide for human groups is bound up with care for other organisms, and both aim to ensure that nature has its share: one by excluding human activity, and the other by making space for all at a shared table.

5. Beyond Demeaning Stereotypes, toward Common Humanness

The scarred and fatigued bodies of the middle-aged men featured here testify to their contribution to regional economies, and to the failure of those economies to reciprocate with care. Norms of subordinate masculinity into which they had been cast involve expectations that men will endure violence in and beyond the workplace, and will perpetuate violence against women, children, other men, and against nature.

Across Latin America, early deaths suffered by low-income men have contributed to growing gaps in life expectancy, where men, on average, have fallen far behind women (Paulson 2015). How are these outcomes related to the massive expansion of ecologically destructive industries such as logging, mining, petroleum, and industrial farming? Among other forces, violent regimes of masculinity have been motivated to justify degrading and hazardous working conditions, and to fuel environmental struggles in which some marginalized men are conscripted into public or private security forces to fight against other marginalized men in conflicts over territory and resources.

While traditions of green primitivism construe indigenous people as naturally closer to nature, and some eco-feminist visions endow women with innate nurturing capacities (Leach 2007), men like these are rarely protagonists of conservation narratives. On the contrary, men described here are publicly condemned as threats to the endangered biodiversity of Brazil's Atlantic Forest, and to private property controlled by the region's socioeconomic elite.

Here we have presented a curious case in which landless men with little formal education, branded as violent destroyers of nature, affirmatively reconstruct life-worlds through nurturing relationships with land, trees, and other features of their biophysical world, as well as with each other. Their lives still involve harsh challenges, and their expressions of masculinity continue to embrace conventional roles as *producers* and *providers*. Yet, even in the face of violent norms and structural domination, these men have managed to expand and enjoy identities as *reproducers* and *caretakers*. That amazing feat, and its sweet rewards, should motivate readers in diverse other contexts.

6. Toward Convivial Futures

In a world where political economic processes continue to undermine ecosystems and communities, and development initiatives continue to focus on expanding money-earning opportunities, efforts to protect the environment will continue to employ closed conservation areas. Some conservation scientists and practitioners will continue to argue that efforts to improve material conditions for people jeopardize the preservation of biodiversity (Sanderson/Redford 2003). We hope that the case presented here will contribute to complementary policies and projects designed to strengthen diverse life-worlds by supporting meaningful and caring relationships among humans and with other nature.

Shifts from political ecologies of mutual violence and degradation toward dynamics of mutual flourishing show that convivial futures are possible, and that struggles for more equal distributions of the means of (re)production play a vital role in such transitions. Interspecies relations of care glimpsed in Peru and Brazil suggest broader possibilities for renewal of the convivial *principle of common naturality*, even among humans who have been marked and rendered as threats to nature.

Against historical conditions in which subordinate men have been brutally employed in the aggressive exploitation of nature for someone else's profit, we find hope in practices and meanings through which some men nurture and care for themselves, others, and non-human nature. Here *principles of common humanity* encourage respect for all fellow humans, even those maligned as violent and destructive.

This is not a story of individual achievement. In the cases we have studied, values and practices that guide people to work and to care in solidarity are rooted in deep *traditions of common sociality*. Continual (re)generation and adaptation of cultural resources and community ties are vital to sustaining shared natural environments.

To support conditions in which these principles can thrive, political economic systems must be reoriented away from domination and growth and toward equitable wellbeing and resilience. And diverse communities must be strengthened in their own collaborative and intergenerational efforts to build life-worlds that seek and celebrate human-environmental wellbeing and justice.

Literature

Agrawal, Arun/Redford, Kent H. (2009): "Conservation and Displacement: An Overview," in: Conservation and Society 7 (1), pp. 1–10.

Brockington, Dan/Duffy, Rosaleen/Igoe, James (2008): Nature Unbound: Conservation, Capitalism and the Future of Protected Areas, London: Earthscan.

Büscher, Bram et al. (2017): "Half-Earth or Whole Earth? Radical Ideas for Conservation, and Their Implications," in: Oryx 51 (3), pp. 407–410.

Büscher, Bram/Fletcher, Robert (2020): The Conservation Revolution: Radical Ideas for Saving Nature Beyond the Anthropocene, London/New York: Verso.

Canal Agroecologia (2020): "Guardiões do Sertão: Eduardo Emidio, Décadas de Inovações Agroflorestais na Caatinga." Available from: https://www.youtube.com/watch?v=CSFa68JvNkE [accessed 8/15/2021].

Convivialist International (2020): "The Second Convivialist Manifesto: Towards a Post-Neoliberal World," in: Civic Sociology 2020 (1), pp. 1–24. Available from: https://doi.org/10.1525/001c.12721 [accessed 8/15/2021]. (= *SCM*)

Dean, Warren (1995): With Broadax and Firebrand: The Destruction of the Brazilian Atlantic Forest, Berkeley: University of California Press.

DeVore, Jonathan Daniel (2014): Cultivating Hope: Struggles for Land, Equality, and Recognition in the Cacao Lands of Southern Bahia, Brazil. Dissertation, University of Michigan.

DeVore, Jonathan Daniel (2017): "Trees and Springs as Social Property: A Perspective on Degrowth and Redistributive Democracy from a Brazilian Squatter Community," in: Journal of Political Ecology 24 (1), pp. 644–666.

DeVore, Jonathan Daniel (2018): "Scattered Limbs: Capitalists, Kin, and Primitive Accumulation in Brazil's Cacao Lands, 1950s–1970s," in: The Journal of Latin American and Caribbean Anthropology 23 (3), pp. 496–520.

DeVore, Jonathan Daniel /Hirsch, Eric/Paulson, Susan (2019): "Conserving human and other nature: A curious case of convivial conservation from Brazil," in: Anthropologie et Sociétés 43 (3), pp. 31–58.

Haraway, Donna (2016): Staying with the Trouble: Making Kin in the Chthulucene, Durham: Duke University Press.

Hirsch, Eric (2017): "The Unit of Resilience: Unbeckoned Degrowth and the Politics of (Post)development in Peru and the Maldives," in: Journal of Political Ecology 24 (1), pp. 462–475.

Leach, Melissa (2007): "Earth Mother Myths and Other Ecofeminist Fables: How a Strategic Notion Rose and Fell," in: Development and Change 38 (1), pp. 67–85.

Paulson, Susan (2015): Masculinities and Femininities in Latin America's Uneven Development, New York: Routledge.

Sanderson, Steven E./Redford, Kent (2003): "Contested relationships between biodiversity conservation and poverty alleviation," in: Oryx 37 (4), pp. 389–390.

Singh, Neera (2017): "Becoming a Commoner: The Commons as Sites for Affective Socio-Nature Encounters and Co-Becomings," in: Ephemera: Theory and Politics in Organization 17 (4), pp. 751–776.

Wilson, Edward O. (2016): Half-Earth: Our Planet's Fight for Life, New York/London: Liveright.

A Convivialist Solution for the Multiple Crisis of Biodiversity, Climate, and Public Health

Tanja Busse

We are facing multiple crises, but so far only the climate crisis has triggered public debates. The global loss of biodiversity is still largely considered to be a minor problem that for most people does not require a profound transformation of the economy and their lifestyles. Yet, as early as 1997 the Union of Concerned Scientists, founded by the Nobel laureate Henry Kendall, tried to raise awareness of this issue. In their *Warning to Humanity*, this group (Union of Concerned Scientists 1997: 1) wrote that the irreversible loss of species might lead to "unpredictable collapses of critical biological systems." Unfortunately, there was nothing but rhetorical reaction to the warning. In 2017, more than 15,000 scientists repeated Kendall's alert. In their *Warning to Humanity: A Second Notice*, they wrote that no problem except for the restoration of the ozone layer had been solved in the meantime. "Moreover, we have unleashed a mass extinction event, the sixth in roughly 540 million years, wherein many current life forms could be annihilated or at least committed to extinction by the end of this century" (Ripple et al. 2017: 1026). Two years later, the Intergovernmental Science-Policy Platform on Biodiversity and Ecosystem Services (IPBES) stated that one million species were likely to go extinct within the next few decades (IPBES 2019). Despite all this scientific weight, most people are still unaware of the importance of the continuing loss of biodiversity and its consequences for life on Earth (Busse 2019: 115 ff.).

There is another global crisis that is still not getting enough attention: a global food and nutrition crisis. It is not only hunger that is making people sick but also the very food they eat. Even though on a global level enough food (as calculated in calories) is produced for everyone, billions of people are malnourished or even suffering from famine. Global warming will change that for the worse. At the same time, there has been an enormous increase of diet-related diseases combined with an obesity epidemic, mostly in industrialized countries. More and more people are eating too much food, too much salt, too much sugar, and too little dietary fiber. Most of these people are living in affluent societies, and yet the choices they make for their diets make them ill. This is not, as the media too often suggest, an individual weakness of character. It is rather a structural problem that is causing this enormous increase in diet-related diseases such as diabetes, cardiovascular problems, and obesity. Neoliberal consumer societies encourage people to buy unhealthy foods, and too many people simply do not have enough time, knowledge, or money to prepare fresh and healthy dishes. Public health experts call this an obesogenic environment.

The global food system plays a crucial role in all three of these crises. Industrial agriculture and especially the mass production of meat is responsible for about a quarter of the global greenhouse gas (GHG) emissions. Even if fossil fuel emissions were to be halted, the greenhouse gases caused by the global food system alone would make it impossible to limit warming to 1.5 degrees Celsius (Clark 2020).

Industrial agriculture is also responsible for the loss of biodiversity across large parts of the world. The United Nations Environment Programme (UNEP) has called the global food system the primary driver of biodiversity loss (UN Environment Programme 2021). It is the global demand for meat that has led to massive land-use changes in Brazil, where rainforests have been destroyed to make space for the production of soybeans, which are used to make biodiesel fuel and as animal feed for livestock in Europe and China. Large portions of the rainforests of South-East Asia have been cleared to create plantations of oil palms because the industry has a huge demand for palm oil as a cheap and convenient ingredient for processed food and care products.

The global food system is controlled by a very few global players. Just four of them—ADM, Bunge, Cargill, Dreyfus—dominate the global commodity markets, and three of them—Corteva, ChemChina/Syngenta, Bayer/Monsanto—control the seed and pesticide production. There are even multispecies animal breeding companies with large shares in the global markets. All of these companies have economic and political influence that has hindered ecological reforms. Farmers throughout the world have lost their independence.

1. Diversity in the Fields and on the Plates

The crises of biodiversity, climate change, and nutrition are deeply interlinked. This offers a huge chance for multi-solution policies that could simultaneously help to produce healthy food and beautifully diverse landscapes with a rich biodiversity and soils that act as carbon sinks (Herren/Haerlin/IAASTD+10 Advisory Group [eds.] 2020). In January 2021, together with the British think tank Chatham House and the NGO Compassion in World Farming, the UNEP launched a report that calls for a transformation of the global food system to support biodiversity (Benton 2021). These organizations propose a shift to more plant-heavy diets, the restoration of whole ecosystems, and a shift from monoculture to more diverse crops—which could make both human food and ecosystems healthier.

The EAT-Lancet Commission, an international team of medical experts and earth-system researchers, has made a very similar proposal for the question of how to produce healthy food for ten billion people in the year 2050 without risking the health of the planet. Their concept of planetary health includes both humans and the biosphere that we depend on, that is, clean air and water, fertile soils, and biodiversity. For them, food is the most important driver to improve both human health and the environment. The planetary health diet that the EAT-Lancet Commission has proposed consists of less sugar and red meat and more fruit, vegetables, legumes, and nuts compared to the today's food consumption in most Western countries. The basic idea is that more diversity in the fields can help to support biodiversity and can also deliver more diversity on the plates.

2. Agroecology as an Ecological and Social Solution

A reimagined agricultural system is another important change to bring about a convivial future. This is because supporting biodiversity in our fields and diversity on our plates can also support the increase in humus content of the soils. There are a number of scientists and farmers throughout the world who are experimenting with a more diverse agriculture that does not harm ecosystems but works symbiotically with nature instead. They try to combine sustainable farming systems such as organic farming or permaculture with the protection of wildlife and ecosystems. Agroforestry, which is the smart combination of fields and pastures and trees and shrubs that are also used to produce food or animal feed, is a good example of this.

The umbrella name for all these ideas is *agroecology*. This approach comprises not only the linkage between agriculture and ecosystems but also the protection of rural livelihoods, social wellbeing, and the rights of peasants. Agroecology thus can be seen as a multi-dimensional approach that tries to combine social and ecological solutions. This makes it quite the opposite of agro-industrial farming, with its hierarchical structures where exploitation of farm laborers and also of farmers is common. In Germany, for example, there are plenty of farmers who are working as independent entrepreneurs but are completely dependent on companies in the 'big meat' industry that determine the conditions of, say, what breed, feed, and medical treatment they have to use as well as the price for their livestock. This kind of agriculture is based on standardized farming systems, on specialization, monoculture or close crop rotations, and a high degree of reliance on technology. It is a system where the principles of industry have been applied to agriculture. To begin farming, young farmers have to invest huge amounts of money, which makes it nearly impossible for them to change their farming system once they have chosen one. This system minimizes the independence of the farmers. They are forced to meet the demands of the big companies or traders. As the so-called modern farmers do not produce unique and special food for local customers but rather commodities for global markets, they depend on the global market price. Their products are replaceable. The global food companies buy commodities irrespective of where they were grown. For them, wheat is wheat regardless of whether it comes from the fertile Magdeburger Börde in Saxony-Anhalt or from the Ukrainian black earth. And chicken is chicken no matter where it was raised; South-East Asia is as good as Lower Saxony. Most consumers end up accepting whatever supermarkets offer. They buy standardized food that is not at all linked to the soil where it was grown. The supermarkets do not tell their costumers about ecosystems and ecological and social diversity. Instead they present their products as if they had no history and no link to the biosphere. In fact, most citizens would agree that the orangutan has to be saved from extinction, yet their consumption of processed food and care products containing palm oil makes them accomplices in the destruction of the orangutan's habitat.

All this makes it quite clear that the triple crises of biodiversity, climate, and nutrition cannot be solved by technological fixes. Rather, there is a need for social changes and different economic rules and structures. Most companies that are addressing ecological challenges are aiming at higher efficiency in their production processes (e.g., more yield per acre with less input, more meat per animal with less feed), but these improvements do not solve the structural problems that cause the extinction of species and livelihoods at the same time.

This is why agroecology can be seen as a model for a convivialist food production. It is a holistic approach that includes biodiversity, climate action, health, fair rules, and participation in decision-making processes for farmers, agricultural workers, producers, and consumers—and all of it mostly on a local level.

3. Food Sovereignty as a Convivial Concept

As it happens, there are projects all over the world that are working on the realization of agroecological ideas. Most of them follow the ideas of convivialism even though the people might not be familiar with the concept and do not use the term. The international peasants' movement

La Vía Campesina coined the term *food sovereignty*, which comes very close to the concept of convivialism. It is used as an alternative term to *food security*, which means that all people should at all times have access to sufficient and safe food (International Food Policy Research Institute 2021). Food sovereignty, by contrast, means that the very people who produce, distribute, and consume food also determine which food is produced and how. So, in a simplified sense, food security would involve a sack of rice being delivered to hungry people, whereas food sovereignty would involve these same people having access to land, water, and other resources to produce their own food, which may or may not be rice. This is a question of empowerment of local communities, and it needs strict rules to be realized. In the Global South, peasants often lose the land they have been cultivating for generations because they have no formal claim to it. As a result, they cannot reclaim their land when governments decide to give it to investors. Food sovereignty is also of great significance to farmers in industrialized countries. Their right to produce organic food is threatened when other farmers use genetically modified seeds or pesticides that are banned in organic farming. Both seeds and pesticides can be transported from one field to the other and ruin the organic farmers' harvest. Corporate patent law threatens the traditional rights of farmers to reproduce their own seeds. And, of course, the economic power of big companies makes it very hard for farmers to gain access to markets. The global corporate food regime limits food sovereignty.

4. Food Policy Councils and Agriculture in Solidarity

If we follow the ideas of agroecology and food sovereignty, what would a convivialist food system look like? Food policy councils in which farmers, fishers, growers, and consumers organize the production and distribution of local food on a grassroots level are a good starting point. The idea was born in the 1980s in the United States and then spread to many countries. In Germany, the first of these councils, or *Ernährungsräte*, were founded more than 20 years later, but in recent years the movement has gained a great deal of influence, having grown to comprise more than 45 councils and a nationwide network (Netzwerk der Ernährungsräte 2021). So far, only a few *Ernährungsräte* have gained anything like transformative power, and this has mostly taken place where local governments have supported the organizations' volunteers, but the idea of linking producers and consumers is nevertheless essential for any transformation. These food policy councils remind the municipalities to develop their own food policy—a task that has been neglected in the era of the corporate food regime where food policy was limited to the provision of space for local supermarkets. In this regard, the city of Copenhagen in Denmark is a European pioneer, followed by Berlin. Both cities use public procurement of food for public cafeterias to strengthen the demand for regional organic food and to facilitate access to healthy food for school children and public employees.

Another starting point for a convivialist food system is community supported agriculture (CSA) or solidary agriculture (*Solidarische Landwirtschaft*, *Solawi*) as it is called in Germany. CSA consists of a group of consumers and farmers who operate a farm together. The basic idea is that instead of buying products, the consumers pay a monthly contribution to the farm, often depending on the individuals' budgets. The group also takes part in decision-making processes as well as some of the farm work itself, and it shares the risks of production. In May 2021, the nationwide Netzwerk Solidarische Landwirtschaft had more than 360 members.

5. Regional Councils for Food and Biodiversity

With so many people already engaged in food policy councils or CSAs and other new models for agriculture and food production, there is already a considerable amount of experience and knowledge to support a convivialist food system. There are enough projects to learn from.

It is the dominance of the corporate food system, entrenched by the set of established funding policies and laws, that is preventing major change. What is needed now is a political process to scale up the impact of these pioneering initiatives and to kickstart the necessary socio-ecological transformation. As a new convivialist food system has to respond to multiple crises, a great deal of expertise will be needed.

But this is not enough. Convivial food also needs a new conception of nature and the way humans relate to their environment. As Jason Moore (2016) has explained, the idea of nature being a simple resource that humans can exploit as they like without providing anything in exchange has a long tradition in capitalism and beyond. What we need in the future is a conception of us humans being a small part of the web of life that we must not destroy if we want to survive. This "common naturality," as the *Second Convivialist Manifesto* calls it (Convivialist International 2020: 7 et passim), is not easy to experience for citizens of industrialized countries who have been trained in human supremacy, speciesism, and the exploitation of natural resources. We need a process of re-learning how to conceive of ourselves as part of the web of life or, as Donna Haraway (2016) puts it, being entangled with all the other living beings.

Indigenous peoples who have not lost sight of their roots might help us gain this understanding, as could some earth-system scientists or ecologists as well as peasants in Western countries who have resisted the industrialization of agriculture. Surmounting the humans-versus-nature dichotomy would be a good starting point to overcome a corporate food system that has severed the links between people and their food.

My proposal is to establish regional councils where farmers, market gardeners, fruit growers, bakers, butchers, and chefs meet experts on climate adaptation and mitigation, public health, ecology, nature conservation, water management, finance, urban and spatial planning, and education, as well as citizens. They should develop a vision of a fair food system that delivers ecosystem services as well as healthy food and also the necessary knowledge about the process of transformation into this new convivialist model. This idea is similar to the economy of common goods that proposes a citizens' convention to democratize the economy by enabling citizens to take part in economic decision-making and to redefine the goals of economy (Felber 2018; Felber 2019). The regional councils for food and biodiversity would bring more expertise to these conventions. Ecologists should explain what kind of biodiversity was lost in the particular region and what kind of land use is needed to re-establish it. Climate scientists and water-management experts should explain the opportunities for carbon sinks and what has to be done to protect the drinking water reserves. Food producers have to explain what they need to produce food for the particular region on this basis to have a fair income. Public canteens and restaurants should be linked as closely as possible to local farms and market gardens. Partnerships between schools and farms should help to children to learn where their food comes from and how it is interlinked with ecosystem services.

Of course, a great deal of public funding will be needed to start and run this process. But more importantly, the system of political regulations has to be adjusted, because currently it allows individuals and companies to make private profits by causing environmental and social harm. This has to be changed as soon as possible. A large number of proposals have been made to compel the internalization of external costs or put the *polluters pay* principle into effect—for example, by introducing a sugar tax, meat tax, pesticide fee, or putting a price tag on carbon emissions. What is also needed are simple regulatory laws that prohibit deceptive advertising and harming animals in nature. These laws also have to be applied to imported products.

But, of course, a convivial food system comprises more than a new set of rules. The basic idea would be to link people to the food they eat and re-establish a shared responsibility among people to value the landscape they live in, the food they eat, and the environment they create together.

Literature

Benton, Tim G. et al. (2021): Food System Impacts on Biodiversity Loss: Three Levers for Food System Transformation in Support of Nature, London: Chatham House.

Busse, Tanja (2019): Das Sterben der anderen: Wie wir die biologische Vielfalt noch retten können, München: Blessing.

Clark, Michael A. et. al. (2020): "Global food system emissions could preclude achieving the 1.5° and 2°C climate change target," in: Science 370 (6517), pp. 705–708. Available from: https://science.sciencemag.org/content/370/6517/705 [accessed 8/15/2021].

Convivialist International (2020): "The Second Convivialist Manifesto: Towards a Post-Neoliberal World," in: Civic Sociology 2020 (1), pp. 1–24. Available from: https://doi.org/10.1525/001c.12721 [accessed 8/15/2021].

Felber, Christian (2018): Fragenkatalog an den Demokratischen Wirtschaftskonvent. Available from: https://web.ecogood.org/media/filer_public/c0/2c/c02c65f3-d63e-45d2-852d-49eea8ca1285/fragenkatalog_an_den_wirtschaftskonvent_tb_gwo_2018.pdf [accessed 8/15/2021].

Felber, Christian (2019): Change Everything: Creating an Economy for the Common Good, London: Zed Books.

Haraway, Donna (2016): Staying with the Trouble: Making Kin in the Cthulucene, Durham: Duke University Press.

Herren, Hans R./Haerlin, Benedikt/IAASTD+10 Advisory Group (eds.) (2020): Transformation of Our Food Systems. The Making of a Paradigm Shift, Berlin. Available from: https://www.weltagrarbericht.de/fileadmin/files/weltagrarbericht/IAASTD-Buch/PDFBuch/BuchWebTransformationFoodSystems.pdf [accessed 8/15/2021].

IPBES (2019): Summary for Policymakers of the Global Assessment Report on Biodiversity and Ecosystem Services of the Intergovernmental Science-Policy Platform on Biodiversity and Ecosystem Services. Bonn. Available from: https://ipbes.net/sites/default/files/2020-02/ipbes_global_assessment_report_summary_for_policymakers_en.pdf [accessed 8/15/2021].

International Food Policy Research Institute (2021): Topic: Food Security. Available from: https://www.ifpri.org/topic/food-security#::text=Food%20security,%20as%20defined%20by,an%20active%20and%20healthy%20life [accessed 8/15/2021].

Moore, Jason W. (ed.) (2016): Anthropocene or Capitalocene? Nature, History, and the Crisis of Capitalism, Oakland: Kairos.

Netzwerk der Ernährungsräte (2021): Ernaehrungsraete. Available from: https://ernaehrungsraete.org [accessed 8/15/2021].

Ripple, William J. (2017): "World Scientist's Warning to Humanity: A Second Notice," in: BioScience 67 (12), pp. 1026–1028. Available from: https://academic.oup.com/bioscience/article/67/12/1026/4605229 [accessed 8/15/2021].

UN Environment Programme (2021): "Our Global Food System Is the Primary Driver of Biodiversity Loss," London. Available from: https://www.unep.org/news-and-stories/press-release/our-global-food-system-primary-driver-biodiversity-loss [accessed 8/15/2021].

Union of Concerned Scientists (1997): World Scientist's Warning to Humanity, Cambridge, MA. Available from: https://www.ucsusa.org/sites/default/files/attach/2017/11/World%20Scientists%27%20Warning%20to%20Humanity%201992.pdf [accessed 8/15/2021].

The Post-Development Agenda
Paths to a Pluriverse of Convivial Futures

Federico Demaria, Ashish Kothari

1. Transformative Alternatives to Development to Envision Convivial Futures

2022 marks the 30th anniversary of *The Development Dictionary* edited by Wolfgang Sachs (1992). While the *Dictionary* might have fallen short of its intention to write the obituary of development, it did send shockwaves through the activist, policy, and scholarly worlds and became an influential text. The relevance and impact of Sachs' book is still felt today. At the same time, there is no dearth of newly revitalized hegemonic notions, with the *amoeba concept* (meaning its high malleability) of sustainable development still being floated and indeed given new life by the global intergovernmental agreement on Sustainable Development Goals in 2015 (United Nations 2015). It was in this context that we published *Pluriverse: A Post-Development Dictionary* (Kothari et al. 2019), which, while emulating the spirit of the original *Dictionary*, brings both reincarnated worldviews and fresh alternatives to the notion of 'development' sharply into view. The starting point is the need to go beyond critique and concentrate efforts that articulate the narratives of those struggling to retain or create diverse ways of life against the homogenizing forces of development. There is a need for radical post-development practices, ideas, and worldviews to become an agenda for activists, policymakers, and scholars to help in truly *transforming our world* and therefore offer an alternative to the 2030 Agenda for Sustainable Development.

The descriptor *post-development* is generally meant as an era or approach in which development is no longer the central organizing principle of social life. Even as critiques of development increase in academic spaces, they are arising with equal power amongst indigenous peoples, local communities, women's rights movements, and other civil-society actors—most prominently amongst the victims of development. Across the world, this is resulting in the resurfacing of ancient worldviews with fresh relevance or in new frameworks and visions that present systemic alternatives for human and planetary wellbeing. It is also forcing the decolonization of knowledge systems and epistemologies, breaking down many of the dualisms that Western patriarchal paradigms have engendered, such as between humans and nature.

Post-development is related to at least four other emerging imaginaries, that of post-capitalism (questioning capitalism's ability or attempt to fully and naturally occupy the economy, with the concomitant visualization of an array of diverse and alternative economic practices), post- or degrowth (decentering growth from the definition of both the economy and social life), post-patriarchy (challenging the primacy of masculinist approaches to political leadership, moral authority, social privilege, and the control of property), and post-colonialism (the critical study of the legacy of colonialism and imperialism, focusing on the human consequences of the control and exploitation of colonized people and their lands). The current mood is "to search for alternatives in a deeper sense, that is, aiming to break away from the cultural and ideological bases of development, bringing forth other imaginaries, goals, and practices" (Gudynas/Acosta 2011: 75; our translation).

Therefore, we argue that the time is ripe to deepen and widen a research, dialogue, and action agenda on a variety of worldviews and practices relating to our collective search for an ecologically wise and socially just world. These should be transformative alternatives to the currently dominant processes of globalized development, including its structural roots in modernity, capitalism, state domination, patriarchy, and more specific phenomena, such as casteism, which are still found in many parts of the world. Plus, they should go beyond the superficial or false solutions that those in power are proposing in an attempt to 'greenwash' development, including variants of the 'green economy,' market remedies, and technofixes. The post-development agenda should investigate the what, how, who, and why of all that is transformative, and what and who is not. Equally, though, proponents of post-development need to overcome a number of weaknesses in their narrative, acknowledge that development as an idea has not been buried, and sharpen their focus on the structural changes needed to deal with issues of inequity, injustice, deprivation, and ecological collapse (Ziai 2015).

The exploration of alternatives to development already finds concrete expression in a panoply of new or re-emerging concepts and practices such as *buen vivir*, convivialism, degrowth, ecological *swaraj*, radical feminisms of various kinds, *ubuntu*, commoning, solidarity economy, and food and energy sovereignty (Kothari/Demaria/Acosta 2014). These are perhaps the most visible examples of an emergent post-developmentalist epistemic-political field towards a pluriverse. These radical alternatives are becoming not only more visible but, increasingly, genuinely credible and viable. And yet they are still marginal in comparison to the dominant narrative and practice of development. Thus, it seems a good moment to make such alternatives more widely known and to facilitate bridges among them while respecting their geopolitical and epistemic specificities. It is also critical to build bridges between constructive alternatives and peoples' movements that are resisting the dominant economic and political systems (Kothari et al. 2019; see also Global Tapestry of Alternatives 2021).

2. Critique of Development and Origins of Alternative Worldviews

A range of different and complementary notions or worldviews have emerged in various regions of the world that seek to envision and achieve more fundamental transformation than that proposed by sustainable development approaches. Some of these are a revival of the long-standing worldviews of indigenous peoples; still others have emerged from recent social and environmental movements in relation to old traditions and philosophies. Arising as they do from different cultural and social contexts, they sometimes differ on their prescriptions (what shall be done and how) but they share the main characteristics of the diagnosis (what is the problem and who is responsible for it) as well as similar or equivalent *Weltanschauungen* ("worldviews").

Unlike sustainable development, which is a concept based on an assumed or forced consensus, these alternative approaches cannot be reduced to any single one and therefore do not aspire to be adopted as a common goal by the United Nations, the OECD, or the African Union. These ideas have been born as proposals for radical change from the local to the global level. Under post-political conditions, they intend to repoliticize the debate on the much-needed socio-ecological transformation, thereby affirming dissent with the current world representations and searching for alternative ones. Along these lines, they are a critique of the current development hegemony, which means they are a critique of the homogenization of cultures as a result of the widespread adoption of particular technologies and consumption and production models experienced in the Global North (Escobar 1995). The Western development model is a mental construct adopted by the rest of the world that needs to be deconstructed. Development might thus be seen as a toxic term to be rejected and thus 'sustainable development' as an oxymoron.

Deconstructing development opens the door for a multiplicity of new and old notions and worldviews or a matrix of alternatives (Latouche 2009). This includes *buen vivir*, a way of life with different names and varieties in various regions of South America; *ubuntu*, with its emphasis on human mutuality in South Africa and several equivalents in other parts of Africa; *swaraj*, which has a focus on self-reliance and self-governance, in India; and many others. What is important is that, while these worldviews are ancient, they are re-emerging in their original or modified forms as a part of the narrative of movements that are struggling against development and/or asserting alternative forms of well-being. Ecofeminist arguments represent a further strand in this post-development rainbow (Salleh 1997).

These worldviews are part of a long search for and practice of alternative ways of living forged in the furnace of humanity's struggle for emancipation and enlightenment *within* (rather than outside of) the womb of nature. What is remarkable about these alternative proposals, however, is that they often arise from traditionally marginalized groups. These worldviews are different from dominant Western ones as they emerge from non-capitalist communities or from non-capitalist spaces such as the household sector in the Global North. They are therefore independent of the anthropocentric and androcentric logic of capitalism, the dominant civilization, as well as with the various state socialist (effectively state capitalist) models that have existed until now. Other approaches emerging from within the industrialized countries—the belly of the beast, so to speak—can also break from dominant logic, such as is the case with degrowth, an example of a non-occidentalist West (Demaria et al. 2013; D'Alisa/Demaria/Kallis 2014; Kallis et al. 2020).

These worldviews differ sharply from today's notion of development. It is not about applying a set of policies, instruments, and indicators to exit 'underdevelopment' and reach that desired condition of 'development.' In any case, how many countries have actually achieved development? Decades after the notion of 'development' spread around the world, only a handful of countries can be called 'developed,' others are struggling to emulate them, and all are doing this at enormous ecological and social costs. The problem is not in the lack of implementation but rather in the concept of development as linear, unidirectional material and financial growth. And if 'development' is seen in its original meaning of the opening up of opportunities and horizons, then what the world is experiencing is widespread 'bad development,' including in those countries regarded as industrialized (e.g., countries whose lifestyle was to serve as a benchmark for backward countries). The functioning of the global system is itself a 'bad developer.'

In short, it is urgent to abandon the conventional concept of progress in its productivist drift and of development (as well as its many synonyms) as a unidirectional concept, especially in its mechanistic view of economic growth. However, it is not only about discarding these. Different views are required, much richer in content as well as in complexity. As Kallis (2015) explains:

> "Sustainable development and its more recent reincarnation 'green growth' depoliticize genuine political antagonisms between alternative visions for the future. They render environmental problems technical, promising win–win solutions and the impossible goal of perpetuating economic growth without harming the environment."

Therefore, these alternative approaches are necessary to challenge the ideas of sustainable development and the associated belief in economic growth as a desirable path in political agendas. They are also important in presenting to us a set of ethical values and principles that underlie positive, transformative action, such as diversity, solidarity, commons, oneness with nature, interconnectedness, simplicity, inclusiveness, equity and non-hierarchy, pluriversality, and peace.

3. Towards a Pluriverse of Convivial Futures

At a time when neoliberal governments and rampant extractivism brutalize the everyday life of citizens around the world and in particular the Global South, it is crucial that oppositional voices and people's movements engage in a concentrated effort of research, outreach, dialogue, and action, informed by and informing grassroots practice. Resistance is crucial but it is not enough. We need our own narratives. Acts of resistance and regeneration offer hope in the here and now.

The future post-development agenda must expand the inventory of the pluriverse, advance the definition of what the transformative alternatives are, show how they differ from flawed solutions, and also explore how they can be articulated. From this perspective, a future agenda shall address the following questions:

- What do the alternatives to development have in common and how are they different?

- What potential exists for tensions and complementarities, given that the socio-ecological communities from which these alternatives emerge are rooted in specific territories and cultural contexts?
- How could these alternatives to development converge and cross-fertilize while also retaining their identity and uniqueness?
- How can we deal with those worlds that do not want to relate with others, for example, the ethno-nationalist and imperializing worlds, without going against the principles of the pluriverse? Is it possible to do so without resorting to universal criteria (pluriversity versus universality)?
- Faced with global problems and ideologies (such as the discipline of economics), is it necessary to put forward global visions that relativize a whole series of anthropological, social, political, and economic visions and ideas that are considered universal? How could the exploration of this pluriverse of alternatives to development, characterized by varying degrees of radicality and success, contribute to transcending the dominant and globalized sociocultural paradigm of industrial civilization?

This also entails empirical explorations of what we can learn from concrete experiences that make up the past, present, and future of the pluriverse (Kaul et al. forthcoming). These include:

- The study of territorial experiences such as Rojava, Chiapas, Cuba, Bhutan, indigenous societies, and any other relevant initiatives;
- historical territorial experiences and exilic spaces, that is, those areas of social and economic life in which people try to escape from capitalist relations and processes, either territorially or by trying to build structures and practices that are autonomous from capitalist accumulation and social control (e.g., Zomia, Maroons, Makhnovia);
- municipal or radical democracy alternatives (e.g., Marinaleda, Mendha Lekha, Longo Maï, Christiania) and ethnographic studies of experiences of solidarity economies and intentional communities;

- various conceptions of a *good life* as a basis for building concrete alternatives (e.g., *buen vivir, minobimaatisiiwin, bamtaare, tri hita karana, shohoj, kyosei, sentipensar*);
- post-growth and wellness policy initiatives (e.g., New Zealand, Wales, Scotland);
- evaluation of alternatives from a variety of perspectives (ecological, gender, economic, democratic, cultural); and
- how to deal with the problems of differentiated populations (with different interests) and the risk of essentializing the 'cultural alternatives'?

These are just some of the open questions that need attention if we want to move forward convivial futures that rely on pluriversal visions of co-existence beyond neoliberal agendas (Convivialist International 2020).

4. Beyond the One World of the United Nations and Towards "A World Where Many Worlds Fit" of the Zapatistas

This chapter has attempted to briefly lay out both the critique of (sustainable) development as well as the potential and nuances of a post-development agenda. *The Post-Development Agenda* is meant to deepen and widen a research, dialogue, and action agenda for activists, policymakers, and scholars on a variety of worldviews and practices relating to our collective search for an ecologically wise and socially just world. Very similar to the main ideas of convivialism, these are meant to be truly transformative and may be distinguished from false solutions in a number of ways: first, in their attempts to transform the structural roots of a problem along political, economic, social, cultural, and ecological axes; second, in their explicit or implicit questioning of the core assumptions of the development discourse (e.g., growth, material progress, instrumental rationality, the centrality of markets and economy, universality, modernity) and its binaries; and third, in encompassing a radically different set of ethics and values to those that underpin the current system.

In conclusion, these alternatives to development practices and worldviews intend to repoliticize the debate on the much-needed socio-ecological transformation, thereby affirming their dissent with the current world representations (e.g., sustainable development) and searching for alternative ones. They highlight the need to overcome the modern ontology of one world and expand on the multiplicity of possible worlds. As Escobar (2011: 139) argues:

> "The modern ontology presumes the existence of One World—a universe. This assumption is undermined by discussions in TDs [transition discourses], the buen vivir, and the rights of Nature. In emphasizing the profound relationality of all life, these newer tendencies show that there are indeed relational worldviews or ontologies for which the world is always multiple—a pluriverse. Relational ontologies are those that eschew the divisions between nature and culture, individual and community, and between us and them that are central to the modern ontology. Some of today's struggles could be seen as reflecting the defense and activation of relational communities and worldviews [...] and as such they could be read as *ontological struggles*; they refer to *a different way of imagining life*, to another mode of existence. They point towards the pluriverse; in the successful formula of the Zapatista, the pluriverse can be described as 'a world where many worlds fit'."

From here we could start envisioning to articulate those values that could guide our coexistence on this planet "enunciating them in the most general (and therefore shareable) terms possible, ending up expressing them in both particular and plural forms" (Convivialist International 2020: 11).

Literature

Convivialist International (2020): "The Second Convivialist Manifesto: Towards a Post-Neoliberal World," in: Civic Sociology 2020 (1), pp. 1–24. Available from: https://doi.org/10.1525/001c.12721 [accessed 8/15/2021].

D'Alisa, Giacomo/Demaria, Federico/Kallis, Giorgos (eds.) (2014): Degrowth: A Vocabulary for a New Era, London: Routledge.

Demaria, Federico/Schneider, Francois/Sekulova, Filka/Martinez-Alier, Joan (2013): "What is Degrowth? From an Activist Slogan to a Social Movement," in: Environmental Values 22 (2), pp. 191–215.

Escobar, Arturo (1995): Encountering Development: The Making and Unmaking of the Third World, Princeton: Princeton University Press.

Escobar, Arturo (2011): "Sustainability: Design for the pluriverse," in: Development 54 (2), pp. 137–140.

Global Tapestry of Alternatives (2021). Available from: https://globaltapestryofalternatives.org [accessed 8/15/2021].

Gudynas, Eduardo/Acosta, Alberto (2011): "La renovación de la crítica al desarrollo y el buen vivir como alternativa," in: Utopía y Praxis Latinoamericana 16 (53), pp. 71–83.

Kallis, Giorgos (2015): "The Degrowth Alternative." Available from: http://www.greattransition.org/publication/the-degrowth-alternative [accessed 8/15/2021].

Kallis, Giorgos/Paulson, Susan/D'Alisa, Giacomo/Demaria, Federico (2020): The Case for Degrowth, Cambridge, UK: Polity Press.

Kaul, S./Akbulut, Bengi/ Demaria, Federico/Gerber, Julien-François (forthcoming): The Pluriverse in Practice: Delinking from Capitalist Modernity? (= Development and Change, Special Issue).

Kothari, Ashish/Demaria, Federico/Acosta, Alberto (2014): "Buen Vivir, Degrowth, and Ecological Swaraj: Alternatives to Development and the Green Economy," in: Development 57 (3), pp. 362–375.

Kothari, Ashish/Salleh, Ariel/Escobar, Arturo/Demaria, Federico/ Acosta, Alberto (eds.) (2019): Pluriverse: A Post-Development Dictionary, Delhi (India): Authors Up Front/Tulika Books.

Latouche, Serge (2009): Farewell to Growth, London: Polity Press.

Sachs, Wolfgang (ed.) (1992): The Development Dictionary: A Guide to Knowledge and Power, London: Zed Books.

Salleh, Ariel (1997): Ecofeminism as Politics: Nature, Marx and the Postmodern, London/New York: Zed Books/Palgrave.

United Nations (2015): Transforming our World: The 2030 Agenda for Sustainable Development. Available from: https://sustainabledevelopment.un.org/post2015/transformingourworld/publication [accessed 8/15/2021].

Ziai, Aram (2015): "Post-Development: Premature Burials and Haunting Ghosts," in: Development and Change 46 (4), pp. 833–854.

Letter to the End-of-the-World Generation

Débora Nunes

It is in solidarity with you who today view the adult world with apprehension and wonder about the future that I write this text. I ask for your permission to offer my experience as a history teacher and researcher on scenarios for the future, which led me to write the book *Auroville, 2046: After the end of one world*. I am 55 years old, have two children who are young adults, and am witnessing the intense awareness among youth about what awaits us long before they reach my age. The testimonies are touching, and the coronavirus pandemic was an accelerant of this view. If a virus can turn the world upside-down like it did, imagine the scale of damage wrought by the tragedies that scientists have said will come to pass, such as climate change.

I want to start by sharing a visionary episode that happened to a young and brilliant student twenty years ago, who wrote under my supervision a monograph about the urban development of the small alternative community of Capão in the Chapada Diamantina, Brazil. His dedicated and competent work earned him a glowing approval from the jury of the urbanism course at the State University of Bahia. As usual, the supervisor embraced the student, welcoming him to the world of researchers, which he was preparing to enter with evident talent. When I asked him about his plans about a possible master's degree, he surprised me by saying he would live in Capão and probably be a tour guide. Astonished, I told him that he was so intelligent and talented that he should become a teacher, to which he replied with something like, "Dear professor, if I am indeed that smart, I cannot arrange my life to serve this world in decay."

This episode touched me because, although at the time I was leading a large program to encourage conscious consumption in the Brazilian university environment, I had no such clarity about the future. I will therefore approach the subject of the future of young people on the basis of the path of this young student, who is today living a simple and happy life in Capão. If you allow me one piece of advice to begin with, I will say: Do not plan careers and achievements tied to the world as it is—or was, before the pandemic—because it will soon no longer exist, and this choice will not be beneficial for you, nor for life as a whole.

Dealing with the *end of a world* is not an easy task, but I can assure you that if the prospects are gloomy, it is also possible to see light at the end of the tunnel. As the sages of old remind us, after every night there always comes a dawn. If the watchwords of the near future are likely to be *destruction* and *uncertainty*, they will also be joined by *resilience* and *creativity*. When barbarism knocks at the door, we will be forced to increase our resilience and regenerate what is being damaged, and in the face of great imbalance, only cooperation can enable us to be reborn as a civilization. *Cooperation* will also be a watchword of the future, and this is certainly promising, but it will require courage and determination. And it will also call for the development of quintessentially feminine traits, such as caring and acceptance, that build networks of affection, friendships, family, and solidarity with the human family and nature.

Despite the catastrophes that are implicit in the idea of the end-of-the-world generation, this can also be seen as a great liberation for the world's youth. They will be the first generation that will not have to adapt to the world of their parents, a dull option for any young person with imagination. And so many have had their lives and professional careers guided by convenience—whether from the market, with the aim of working where one potentially earns more money, or from prestige, which means following in the family footsteps in order to inherit respect, privileged conditions, and also high remuneration.

These old paths where young people once projected their futures have often resulted in frustrated expectations and unhappiness owing to the betrayal of their individual talents. In any case, the expectation of money and prestige has always been for the few, leaving the overwhelming majority frustrated and unhappy. Now money and prestige have become a chimera accessible perhaps only to a very few young people from families that have managed to save their fortunes despite all the obstacles that they have had to face and thus to finance the *prosperity* of another generation. Throughout history, many young people have had to forsake their talents—not to mention their sexual choices, their artistic inclinations, and their most creative dreams—in order to integrate into their home community. Today, because of the impact of uncertainty, they tend to be freer to choose their paths.

The dreams of *success*, of *successful careers*, of enrichment and prestige, have been stimulated by the capitalist culture that has built the disaster we are witnessing. The market model in which profit is the sole objective is not resilient, especially during such transformative times. In the radical change that the future will surely bring, it is foolish to waste the intelligence and talent of youth on traditional perspectives. In a world to be rebuilt, all the energy and creativity of the young will be very welcome, especially if they accept the future as being uncertain and therefore develop resilience—that ability to accommodate the shocks of life by focusing on the most important things in one's existence: learning, love, a sense of wholeness, and the joys of living and socializing.

Most likely, prosperity will be conceived of differently in the future. It will be much more linked to the idea of being able to recover nature and renew human relationships on a sustainable basis. Producing healthy food, clean water, clean air; reinvigorating soils and forests; and recreating biodiversity—the world's great wealth—will be much more prestigious skills in the future. Building solid human relationships in solidarity with people near and far will be another prestigious skill. Being an artist, bringing to the world more fantasy, unexpected possibilities, deep explorations of the soul ... all of this will be precious and much more valued, giving youth more reasons to rebel, as they have always done, but bringing a new legitimacy: claiming to affirm their service to the world when they do what their soul asks them to do.

The word *uncertainty* will appear much more frequently in our future lives, and we will finally learn how much the desire to control the uncertain is an illusion. It is better to be open to the unforeseen and make the best of it. When systems become destabilized, especially the Earth's natural system, predictions will be more difficult, even with all our technological advances. I thus move on to a second piece of advice, if you will indulge me: I strongly recommend that young people develop their intuition, this human ability that is considered to be feminine, so little used, and even despised. Intuition is a kind of intimate vision, made possible when mind and heart are in tune. It involves body and soul, and with intuition it is possible to choose the best path in the face of fear, uncertainty, and doubt. This ability can be developed through daily exercises when the mind is calmed and other wisdom is put at our service. It will be an important factor in increasing resilience and the serenity needed to listen to greater wisdom in the face of adversity and opportunity. Intuition is also a great friend of creativity and thus of art, science, and invention.

A great potentiality of the future can already be experienced today: learning over the Internet, taking advantage of the spirit of cooperation that reigns there and that is natural in human beings. This spirit of cooperation is widely practiced by many alternative communities. Today, these groupings, of which ecovillages are a shining example, are already engaged in various win–win economic modes of sharing and redistribution; in sustainable ways of dealing with nature to produce food and forests; in integrative modes of education and health that draw on the innate wisdom of children and our bodies to learn and stay healthy; in collaborative practices of self-knowledge that rely on the idea of transforming oneself to transform the world; in the democratic governance of local collectives that inspire transformations on larger scales; in the moderation of consumption required by the zero-waste imperative; in collaborative and ecological open-source technologies, creative commons, and the like.

It is highly likely that in the future there will be many shortages of what was once common as a result of the succession of predictable crises of food, water, and fuel, the volatility of money, restrictions on mobility, and so on. In this case, what was abundant and harmful will fortunately gradually run out: oil, plastics, disposables, waste, superficiality, exacerbated competition, senseless consumption. We will open our eyes to see abundance where it was once invisible. All the possibilities of recycling that transform waste into useful objects will be valued in this future world where dumps and landfills are treasures. And so, what was little valued by the market, what yields little or no money but brings meaning to life, will become essential: restoring broken objects, the arts in general, working with the soil, and simple handmade stuff. Also essential will be that which does not bring any material wealth: contemplation, quietude, deliberate idleness, pleasant and joyful interaction among friends.

Think, dear young people, of the appealing world that may be coming into existence—a world in which the "inner technologies" of Mirra Alfassa's dream for the most important ecovillage, Auroville, become a way forward. The "Mother" of Auroville said that a time would come when we would harmonize our external achievements—the incredible technologies invented by humankind to deal with the outer world—with inner technologies, ingenious and sensitive ways of dealing with our interior worlds. This immense universe that is inside each one of us is interconnected with others and can evolve. This is what Gustav Jung told us in his concept of the collective unconscious, as Rupert Sheldrake tells us today in his concept of morphogenetic fields, or as the ancestral wisdoms have always told us. Evolution moves us towards more lovingkindness, and human history itself proves this if we follow the historical evolution of the idea of the right to a joyful life, for example.

You, the youth of today, can help humanity to make great strides in the direction of lovingkindness. I invite you, dear youth, to open your eyes to see people and communities that have already been living post-capitalism for years and even decades. They bet on learning to live together, as the *Convivialist Manifestos* of our time invite us to do. In fact, these communities have only updated the concepts that were present in the ways of life of the original cultures that were suffocated by colonialism. They understood that harmony between us and the Earth, between ourselves and others, and between the various parts of ourselves—body, soul, heart, and mind—is the only way we can survive together and thrive subjectively and materially. And to be happy and to allow others to be happy too. The world is failing but also starting over, and you will make that history by overcoming not only capitalism but patriarchy too.

Where you are is also going to be especially important for the opportunities that are available to you. Until now big cities and megacities have been the loci of those opportunities, but they are heavy and dependent constructs with extremely low resilience and unsustainable. They are increasingly expensive, polluted, congested, violent, and nothing on the horizon points to this getting better. On the contrary. Medium and small cities, ecovillages, life in the countryside all offer greater resilience to environmental, economic, social, political problems. Having a green belt around a city offers easier access to food, having a government in reach favors democracy, having families and friends nearby favors cooperation, and neighborhood life is much more vibrant in smaller urban spaces.

An economy of proximity is more solid. The shorter circuits, so to speak, strengthen the local economy and distribute income. For this very reason, there will be a tendency toward decentralization even in large cities. With the pandemic and the acceleration of remote work, via digital technologies, millions of people have left the cities and settled in quieter places while maintaining their ability to work and interact. When they had to remain isolated at home, people took much more advantage of local commerce and neighborhood relations. All this is already impacting the future, showing that there are ways out when the accumulation of crises is transforming megacities into places with many more problems than opportunities.

This scarcity of what was abundant and this abundance of what was unexpectedly useful tends to be a feature of the future. As an example, let's think about food and look at something that is already a trend among the most innovative youth: the incredible edibles. You know that hardy little plant that is just around the corner, growing without care? It could be an incredibly tasty, very nutritious edible. When science tells us that climate change will make it increasingly difficult to continue growing the foods we are used to in the places where they have always been grown, this can open our eyes to other nutritious possibilities. This is what is happening in many parts of India today with rice, the national food. Many experiments are being done to replace it with millet, a much more nutritious and climate-resilient grain that requires much less water and provides much more nutrients than rice. Yet it was once despised.

It is when catastrophe becomes anastrophe, reconstruction, that each young person can find the joy in doing what they love and thus serving the world—without choosing a career for prestige and money, as has been done for generations, and without making any other life choices of any kind under the crushing weight of past generations, just being inspired by what they did that you admire and honor. You will be the gardeners of tomorrow, who know how to replenish, who deal with conflicts using your heart and not your bile, who realize that each individual gesture builds the collective world, that your internal world is reflected in the external world. And you will task yourselves with doing the best for yourselves, doing the best for the world. I trust you, and I also wish you good luck. We are in this together.

(Un-)Convivial Futures

Right Here, Right Now
The Art of Living Together

Andrea Vetter, Matthias Fersterer

>In the beginning when the word was spoken,
>in the beginning when the fire was lighted,
>in the beginning when the house was built,
>>we were among you.
>
>Silent, like a word not spoken,
>dark, like a fire not lighted,
>formless, like a house not built,
>>we were among you:
>>>the sold woman,
>>>the enslaved enemy.
>
>We were among you, coming closer,
>>coming closer to the world.
>
>In your time when all the words were written,
>in your time when everything was fuel,
>in your time when houses hid the ground,
>>we were among you.
>
>Quiet, like a word whispered,
>dim, like a coal under ashes,
>insubstantial, like the idea of a house,
>>we were among you:
>>>the hungry,
>>>the powerless,
>>in your world, coming closer,
>>coming closer to our world.

> In the ending when the words were forgotten,
> in the ending when the fires burned down,
> in the ending when the walls fell down,
> > we were among you:
> > > the children,
> > > your children,
> > > dying your dying to come closer,
> > > to come into our world, to be born.
> We were the sands on your sea-coasts,
> the stones of your hearths. You did not know us.
> We were the words you had no language for.
> O our fathers and mothers!
> We were always your children.
> From the beginning, from the beginning,
> > we are your children.
> (Ursula K. Le Guin, *Always Coming Home*)

1. Discarding Convivial Futures

There is no such thing as a *convivial future*. A convivial future is an oxymoron, a contradiction in terms. Conviviality is not about linearity and progress, not about planning and designing a better world for the day after tomorrow; not about aiming at an allegedly better future at the expense of a good here and now; not about drafting blueprints for ideal societies that could be applied in any given context, at any given time, at any given place. On the contrary, *conviviality* refers to a specific kind of lived togetherness that is shared between all the human and non-human inhabitants of a specific place in time: not anywhere, anytime—but right here, right now! Conviviality challenges the very concept of future itself. Paradoxically, as we will argue, it is exactly by abandoning abstract notions of 'the future,' of 'universality,' of humans as 'self-reliant rational beings' and other modes of anthropocentric and utopist thinking that future beings may once be able to lead decent, convivial lives on our home planet and at its countless "centers of the world," as Ursula

K. Le Guin (1989: 82) called localities that are "known and named," that are "not a goal, not a place to get to, but a place where one is."

In the following reflections, we will orbit around ways of envisioning and realizing convivial forms of living here and now as worthy ancestors-to-be for our children—those living and those yet to be born—and our fellow beings. In doing so, we will draw upon ideas formulated by two ancestral accomplices, Ursula K. Le Guin and Ivan Illich.

2. Hidden Premises of Mistrust

Ivan Illich (1973: 11) defined conviviality half a century ago as follows:

> "I intend it to mean autonomous and creative intercourse among persons, and the intercourse of persons with their environment; and this in contrast with the conditioned response of persons to the demands made upon them by others, and by man-made environment. I consider conviviality to be individual freedom realized in personal interdependence and, as such, an intrinsic ethical value."

The editors of this volume aim at collecting "accounts of another future world, one that is attractive to an Italian worker, a Spanish peasant, a farmer in Senegal, an inhabitant of a favela in Rio or a slum in Bombay, an Egyptian employee, an Iraqi doctor, a Chinese student, but also one that a French or German company director would be happy to live in" (see Adloff/Caillé in this volume). What could such a world look like? We suggest that such a world will have to be one, in which many worlds fit, as the Zapatistas famously stated. Envisioning such a *pluriverse* will require ways of thinking that are radically different from those Western political theory has applied for centuries. The goal formulated above as well as convivialist thinking in general could easily be misunderstood as striving for a new kind of world society, as described in the all too familiar contract theories laid down by educated white men, such as Thomas Hobbes or John Rawls three centuries or eight decades ago, respectively. These theories basically state that we were able to find an ideal mode of organizing the world by collectively constructing the blueprint for an ideal society under a 'veil of ignorance.' All human beings—that is the idea—should discuss together which society would be best, given that nobody knows which geographical and social place they would inhabit in such a world. According to Hobbes and Rawls these are the conditions for ensuring a just and equal society.

However, these ideas of society as a contract are diametrically opposed to convivialism. Contract theories rely upon many hidden premises, starting with the notion that people might want to organize themselves by means of contracts. Contracts are very special forms of conceptual artefacts that have evolved around trade activities since the times of ancient Mesopotamia some six millennia ago and, by their very nature, depend on written letters. As anthropologist Marshall Sahlins (1972 [1965]: 191) pointed out, *trade* is a human interaction that occurs between strangers who mistrust each other, whereas in contexts of kin, clan, or friendship completely different forms of distributing and pooling goods and services will be used. Current research on commoning as means of social organization confirms this insight (Helfrich/Bollier 2019).

Something very similar applies to the concept of *contract*: a contract is something to ensure that a given fact negotiated between the parties involved might go on 'forever,' that is, as long as the institutions legitimizing a contract exist, namely a state, a legislative apparatus, and a police force. As David Graeber (2011) showed in *Debt*, his social history of structural economic bondage in Western societies, contracts are predominantly written constructs between people who do not know and who mistrust each other, they are the very foundation of any state bureaucracy's "[u]topia of [r]ules" (Graeber 2015). On a grander level, the social interactions between people who do not know and who mistrust each other have been organized by the large-scale contractual agreements known as *states*. As anthropologist James C. Scott (1998; 2009) argued, statecraft as such is intrinsically intertwined with oppression and structural violence, as any state-making project first needs to make *legible* its subjects. This act of making living people legible as if they were abstract letters or numbers is necessarily connected to social stratification, levelling down, normalization, and, consequently, othering. Any norm is meaningful only insofar as it can be delineated from all the many 'others' who do not comply to the norm. Declaring, for instance, white, male, rationalist, self-interested state subjects to be the norm will create multitudes of 'others' failing to meet this standard.

How, then, can we refer to those other forms of interaction between people who know and trust each other? Looking for a term for "non-market related" activities that "by their very nature escape bureaucratic control," Ivan Illich (1981: 44) suggested to recover the word "vernacular" (from Latin *vernaculum*, referring to "rootedness" and "abode"), designating "whatever was homebred, homespun, homegrown, homemade, as opposed to what was obtained in formal exchange" (ibid.: 57). Bearing in mind that that which is convivial tends to be place-centered and vernacular, we move on with examining another hidden premise.

A contract, as the hidden premise has it, is concluded between allegedly autonomous individuals whose actions are based on rational decision-making and who are accountable to none—neither to clan or kinship nor to human ancestors or the "more-than-human world" (Abram 1997). The contracting persons are de facto modelled in the image of that decrepit chimaera of *homo economicus*: as boundlessly floating individuals who are committed to nothing else but their well understood self-interests. The very idea that all we had to do now was finding a new social contract ensuring that human beings lived together peacefully on a permanent basis without exploiting their fellow beings is bound to come to nothing. For this idea misconstrues the fact that the concept of society-as-a-contract is intrinsically intertwined with the very same imperial lifestyles that it seeks to overcome in the first place.

3. Living Together Artistically rather than Contractually

Fortunately, conviviality points towards a completely different direction: conviviality is a mode of being between people—human or non-human—, that can neither be fixed in juridical codes nor made litigable. This is the core difference between conviviality and contractual agreements made to ensure social justice, equal distribution, and ethnic or gender equality. This is not at all to imply that convivial societies were unjust or unequal—but in convivial societies, justice and equality are based on interconnected, embedded, and context-bound direct social interactions between the people concerned; whereas many contemporary movements for justice and equality are based on the hidden premise of contractual agreements, for example, that universal rights are to be formulated for a global society in the manner of social contracts to be enforced by the agents of structural and physical violence: bureaucracies, judiciary apparatuses, and the police force. Conviviality, however, is not a contract but an art—the "art of living together [*convivere*]," as spelled out in the *Second Convivialist Manifesto* (Convivialist International 2020 [hereafter cited as: *SCM*]: 1 and 7).

Therefore, when deepening the question what a convivial society would look like, the term *conviviality* itself forces us to be very *radical* ("going to the roots"). It urges us to thoroughly consider what a place would look like where living together is an art rather than a contractual agreement. Central elements of living together in this way include talking to each other, telling stories following the oral tradition, playing music, performing rituals, caring for oneself and for the multiple others—be they humans, plants, animals, microbes, rivers, forests, mountains, landscapes, etc. As suggested above, this lifestyle bears on a deep level of commitment and dedication towards a place in time, a center of the world, including all of its inhabitants—instead of being forced by means of bureaucracy to adhere to lifestyles that compel us by their very structure to exploit and harm our fellow beings, often without even noticing it.

The *art* of living together cannot be plotted, pigeonholed, or made legible in a plan, a scheme, or a blueprint, designating isolated bureaucratic sectors, such as *mobility, education, social welfare, environmental protection, distributional justice*, etc. Trying to draw up an education scheme for the year 2050, for instance, is likely to end up in projecting the present onto the canvas of an unknown future—a projection that is bound to be either quite boring, lackluster, and dreary or else exceedingly lofty, ungrounded, and speculative. In any event, such projections of the present onto the future will be based on some of the very same hidden premises that we need to get rid of in order to open the pathway to artistic creation.

Art is inherently interwoven with the notion of culture. Understood in an anthropological sense, culture is the ensemble of rites, norms, and practices that people adhere to at a certain place at a certain time in a certain way that they consider to be common-sense. Culture is a carpet woven jointly by the—ancestral, living, or yet unborn—people of a specific place at a specific time. It is simply not possible to fabricate such a carpet elsewhere or elsewhen and then impose it as a readymade blueprint upon people regardless of their specificity—any attempt to do so has ended up in colonialist, fascist, or other totalitarian forms. Culture simply cannot be woven, unless it is embedded in a *known and named* place and given all the time it needs to unfold its specificity and potentiality. This place-bound approach is closely connected to the term "heterotopia" coined by Michel Foucault (1989 [1984]) to designate a place in time that is alternative insofar as it subverts the ways and rules of normalist mainstream society.

Another hint at the place-centered nature of *culture* lies in the term itself, which is derived from Latin *cultivare* ("tending the soil"). Therefore, by its very essence, culture is intrinsically intertwined with the soil that we tread and feed upon and that we all will return to at the end of our lives, with our physical bodies becoming compost nourishing the plants growing on specific plots of land and our ideas and thoughts becoming threads for the cultural weaving patterns that may evolve into our children's future. People living in such a "becoming-compost" way are aware of the ever changing, non-linear, collaborative, and interdependent multitude that is life on, in, and through earth. Similarly, in her speculative fabulations *Staying with the Trouble*, Donna Haraway (2016) referred to people as "compostists."

This place-centered, becoming-compost attitude is not to be confused with blood-and-soil ideologies. Firstly, acknowledging the complexly immersive process of becoming-compost is completely contrary to any concept of soil as something *static*, *closed*, and *pure*. Secondly, places of conviviality inhabited by people who are embedded in a rich web of interconnected relational structures tend to embrace diversity, inclusiveness, and ambiguity. Ivan Illich's ethical credo "individual freedom realized in personal interdependence" mentioned above forecloses segregating, cruel, or xenophobic ideologies. However, openness, diversity, and hospitality are qualities that have to be constantly tended, cared for, and renewed.

What is more, this unfolding art of living together is something completely different altogether than the search for a *utopia*—an ideal society that in a carrot-and-stick fashion promises to always be looming just beyond the horizon. A utopia (from Greek *ou*, "not," and *tópos*, "place," literally: "non-place") is something that by definition cannot be reached, cannot be located, situated, or grounded, and, by implication, can be applied to any place and no place at all—it is a fool's paradise, a cloud-cuckoo-land, a neverwhere, an abstract ideal, a promise made of very thin air. And yet, it is utopian thinking turning into universalist blueprints that has been at the core of much of Western concepts of progress. Certainly, there is nothing wrong with trying to imagine that which is not here yet—if it were, we would not have seen, for instance, votes for women or the end of slavery—however, things tend to get terribly messy when blueprints of lifestyles taken by some to be good, true, and universal are imposed upon others, regardless of who, where, and when they are.

4. Principles, Patterns, Practices

Let us turn again to the art of conviviality. How, then, can we cultivate at a concrete place in time ways of artfully living together? Where do people cultivate the art of becoming-compost? Can we identify patterns in such jointly woven carpets that may tell us stories about the art of conviviality?

In the *SCM* (7), the following principles of conviviality are spelled out:

> "The only legitimate policies, but also the only acceptable ethics, are those based on the following five principles: common naturality, com-

mon humanity, common sociality, legitimate individuation, creative opposition. These five principles are subordinate to the absolute imperative of hubris control."

This sounds plausible enough. But where do we go from these principles? Are they meant to be the building blocks of yet another social contract, this time for a world society? Or could they be used to form a matrix, a fertile ground, from which patterns informing the art of living together in a becoming-compost sense may sprout?

What is actually the difference between principles and patterns? Whereas a *principle* is a normative guideline for behavior or evaluation, a *pattern* is—like a motive in a carpet—a certain cultural element, which people get inspired by, which they may copy, adapt, and alter according to their respective needs and to their carpets' fabrics. Patterns are not invented but are rather identified, recovered, or mined from phenomenological perception. Patterns do not say what ideal people in an ideal world *ought* to do but rather describe what actual people living at an actual place actually *do* (Alexander 1979). By placing the focus on the ways people organize their lives intrinsically, if they are not prevented from doing so by structures imposed upon them, the practice of finding such patterns subverts the prevalent structures of normalized mainstream and has even visionary potential: it makes us see the potentiality of that which is right here, right now, if only we allow for it to unfold. Drawing upon design thinker Christopher Alexander, commons activists Silke Helfrich and David Bollier (2019) developed the groundwork for a pattern language of commoning. The ways in which patterns are incorporated at a given locality vary from place to place, and so do the rules and regulations necessary to organize a given commons—they are not deducted from abstract universalist norms, values, and ideals but are embedded into regional and social contexts that are vernacular, place-centered, and highly idiosyncratic. As Nobel laureate and commons researcher Elinor Ostrom (2010) famously pointed out: when it comes to organizing commons, "[t]here are no panaceas!"

The units of organization structuring life at places of conviviality tend to be much smaller than many current administrative and bureaucratic units. So what about scalability? The very question whether convivial principles, patterns, and practices emerging from a specific place in time could be applied to other places or units of a larger scale is a categorial mistake and is itself a sign of utopist universalism. What developed at one place may not at all be compatible with another place. However, *heterotopias* will connect with each other to form non-hierarchical, polycentric webworks of idiosyncratic places. They will do so inevitably because human beings are always part of multiple intersecting groups—be they kinship, friendship, love relationships, care relationships, working collectives, etc. A more telling question to be asked would, therefore, be: what are the links, intersections, and common features connecting places of conviviality and what kind of structural and protective features allow for these connections to spread, flourish, and intensify?

But is all that not overly naive? What use is there in people practicing the art of living together and becoming-compost, if the rules of mainstream society and economy urge them to work towards monetary profits, to pay taxes, and to exploit other beings while being part of a world-eating civilizational paradigm? Our intervention is meant as a challenge to the widespread assumption that utopist thinking, which, as we showed, is based on hidden premises, such as universalism, abstraction, rationalism, and linearity, would pave the way towards a better future. If we are to envision a good life for all rather than just keep on replicating the very structures we are trying to overcome, then we need to begin at a different starting point altogether. This is not to say that in the light of existing nation states, international treaties, and a globalized economy it would not be worth fighting on a national and international level for more social justice, more gender equality, or laws protecting human rights and the environment. On the contrary, demonstrating against racist police action and occupying hotspots of financial speculation, nuclear power plants, airport runways, pipelines, or forests scheduled for logging is important! And so is lobbying with social movements and NGOs to alter legislative frameworks in order to end racist, sexist, and anthropocentric oppression.

Although this kind of *compassionate activism* is something quite different from unfolding the art of living together in a becoming-compost fashion both activities are nourished by similar qualities of place-centered embeddedness, vernacular resistance, and kindred connectedness to our fellow beings. Is it possible, however, for a single human being to do both: fighting against oppression and setting up alternative structures of conviviality? Firstly, fighting oppression is not a task a single human being could ever live up to—it takes generations of millions of people. Secondly, interestingly enough, the very places where oppression is fought—be it climate camps, tree sittings at Hambach Forest, or protests at Standing Rock—are often organized as heterotopias. The very action of standing with a tree and protecting it from being cut down to give way to yet another highway may assist human beings in reconnecting to some wider understanding of the way that our breathing mammal bodies are deeply embedded into concrete places and "the web of life" (Moore 2015) itself—nothing else is meant by *conviviality*!

But what about the future? Can we really afford not to work towards a better future in the light of climate crisis, species extinction, and exacerbating social injustice? And if so, what would be the alternative? We will give a tentative answer by resorting to the convivial practice of storytelling. One night, sitting at a campfire, social anthropologist and subsistence researcher Veronika Bennholdt-Thomsen (for her general perspective, see Bennholdt-Thomsen/Mies 2000) told us the following anecdote: while she was doing field research in the Bolivian Andes, a woman from an indigenous community told her: "You Western people are always chasing after a good future. For us it's completely different! We know that our present will turn into our children's past. That's why we make sure to create a good present so that one day we will have a good past that we may cherish together with our children!"

Ursula K. Le Guin (2019 [1985]) even went a step further. Her opus magnum, *Always Coming Home*, giving detailed insights into the convivial styles and manners of a fictitious indigenous people living in a future version of Northern California includes a poem in which the children of the future address us, the people of the present: in an act of turned around intergenerational welfare they console us and encourage us to sow today the seeds from which one day their own convivial present may sprout. In order to do so, we need to be receptive to the shades and shadows that desirable futures may cast here and now instead of trying to cook up, scheme, and construct a purportedly better future in the name of those coming after us, while wrecking the very basis of human life on our planet. This makes all the more sense given the fact that time is perceived as cyclical rather than linear in many indigenous cultures. With this in mind, we kindly invite you to turn back to the beginning: *"In the beginning when the word was spoken …"*

Literature

Abram, David (1996): The Spell of the Sensuous: Perception and Language in a More-Than-Human World, New York: Vintage Books.

Alexander, Christopher (1979): The Timeless Way of Building, Oxford: Oxford University Press.

Bennholdt-Thomsen, Veronika/Mies, Maria (2000): The Subsistence Perspective: Beyond the Globalised Economy, London: Zed Books.

Convivialist International (2020): "The Second Convivialist Manifesto: Towards a Post-Neoliberal World," in: Civic Sociology 2020 (1), pp. 1–24. Available from: https://doi.org/10.1525/001c.12721 [accessed 8/15/2021]. (= *SCM*)

Foucault, Michel (1989 [1984]): "Different Spaces," in: Foucault, Michel: Aesthetics, Method, and Epistemology (= Essential Works of Foucault, 1954–1984 2), ed. by James D. Faubion, New York: The New Press, pp. 175–185.

Graeber, David (2011): Debt: The First 5000 Years, New York: Melville House.

Graeber, David (2015): The Utopia of Rules: On Technology, Stupidity, and the Secret Joys of Bureaucracy, New York: Melville House.

Haraway, Donna J. (2016): Staying with the Trouble: Making Kin in the Chthulucene, Durham: Duke University Press.

Helfrich, Silke/Bollier, David (2019): Free, Fair, and Alive: The Insurgent Power of the Commons, Gabriola Island: New Society.

Illich, Ivan (1973): Tools for Conviviality, New York: Harper & Row.
Illich, Ivan (1981): Shadow Work, Boston/London: Marion Boyars.
Le Guin, Ursula K. (1989): "A Non-Euclidean View of California as a Cold Place to Be," in: Le Guin, Ursula K.: Dancing at the Edge of the World: Thoughts on Words, Women, Places, New York: Grove Press, pp. 80–100.
Le Guin, Ursula K. (2019 [1985]): Always Coming Home, Author's Expanded Version, New York: Library of America.
Moore, W. Jason (2015): Capitalism in the Web of Life: Ecology and the Accumulation of Capital, London: Verso.
Ostrom, Elinor (2010): "No Panaceas! Elinor Ostrom talks with Fran Korten, 27th February 2010," in: Yes Magazine. Available from: www.yesmagazine.org/issue/america-remix/2010/02/27/elinor-ostrom-wins-nobel-for-common-s-sense [accessed 8/15/2021].
Sahlins, Marshall (1972 [1965]): "On the Sociology of Primitive Exchange," in: Sahlins, Marshall: Stone Age Economics, New York: de Gruyter, pp. 185–275.
Scott, James C. (1998): Seeing Like a State: How Certain Schemes to Improve the Human Condition Have Failed, New Haven/London: Yale University Press.
Scott, James C. (2009): The Art of Not Being Governed: An Anarchist History of Upland Southeast Asia, New Haven: Yale University Press.

"2050"
30 Years of Change and Yet No New Beginning

Frank Adloff

Looking back from the year 2050, we can see that many opportunities and shifts were missed to shape coexistence on Earth peacefully, justly, and ecologically within planetary boundaries.[1] A convivial genesis did not take place. Instead we can observe a strong social change full of contradictions, abrupt tipping points, and harsh conflicts. While the 20th century (despite disruptive humanitarian catastrophes in the form of world wars and the Holocaust) still proceeded in the mode of steady social change, it was already apparent at the beginning of the new century that disruption would henceforth characterize social change: The historic upheavals of the terrorist attack of September 11, 2001, the economic and financial crisis of 2008, or the coronavirus pandemic of 2020–21 can be mentioned here like ciphers. With particular regard to the pandemic period, the impression arose in parts of the population around the world that the previously hegemonic project of Western modernity with its narrative of progress had come to an end.

---

1 This report was commissioned by the International Convivialist Association (ICA) in 2050 to determine which processes of social change have been significant over the last 30 years. It is the executive summary.

1. Social, Economic, and Political Divisions

At that time, a rift ran through the imaginary spaces of societies, and it became clear that existing certainties can collapse rapidly. Since then, contingency awareness and the loss of certainties have been hallmarks of the era. New forms of peaceful, fair, and ecologically compatible co-existence seemed to be within reach and have been increasingly implemented in practice in recent decades. But a true, proper new beginning was prevented by increasingly powerful counter-movements that rely on the curtailment of contingencies, defense of privilege, and protection against fear. Fear of the future is the affect of the present in 2050, which many governments and social movements instrumentalize and channel into a quest for power, control, and certainty.

In all fields of social change—economic, political, cultural, technological, and last but not least ecological change, which can no longer be separated from social change—we observe, on the one hand, developments based on path dependencies that have existed for some 50 years or more and, on the other hand, paths that have been disrupted and radical path changes. But rarely for the better.

Since 2020, the structure of economic globalization has changed significantly compared to previous decades. A large number of sectors, above all the financial industry, have been able to maintain and in some cases expand global interdependencies. In contrast, other sectors, dubbed key industries by states, have come under the curatorship of national governments. Capitalism is still susceptible to crises (we recall here the major global economic crises of 2022, 2032, and 2044) but its often predicted end with a post-capitalist new beginning has not yet arrived.

The basic patterns of the global division of labor have remained untouched. Global inequalities between nations persist, and a multitude of negative social and ecological consequences of the imperial way of life of the North continue to be externalized to economically weak and vulnerable countries. Yet, economic alternatives have been steadily gaining ground worldwide. In many social niches around the world, a convivial economy has become established that is regionally oriented, critical of growth (pursuing degrowth instead), oriented towards the common good, and resilient in the face of external economic shocks. However, the potential for the macro-economic transformation of these economic practices is, on the whole, very low, not only because antagonistic economic interests continue to exercise great political influence but also because the alternative economic movement has lacked an intellectually and politically effective network, as was characteristic of neoliberalism in the second half of the 20th century with the Mont Pellerin Society to name but one among many others.

This is accompanied by the continuation of social divisions along the dimensions of income and wealth. Although income inequality has stopped increasing, it has not been possible to effectively combat wealth inequality worldwide. The voices that grew louder after the financial crisis of 2008, calling for effectively fighting wealth inequality, were not able to gain global acceptance in the years that followed. Wealth inequality in Europe as well as in the USA and BRICS states (Brazil, Russia, India, China, and South Africa) has increased steadily, due among other things to tax evasion and new tax havens. There are only a few exceptions: The Scandinavian countries, for example, returned to their egalitarian welfare model in the late 2020s but are pursuing a national strategy of homogenizing their populations and only allowing migration very selectively.

As predicted decades ago, global migration has increased rapidly. Many millions of people are fleeing wars and environmental disasters every year. While there were initially attempts to allow orderly migration to the Global North through asylum procedures, the countries of the North have now completely switched to an approach of containing migration through security policies. The number of refugee camps has increased exponentially since 2026, the year of the great global drought. One reaction to this was the founding of the Mediterranean Union in 2029, the main goal of which has been to fortify Europe's borders to the outside world and to prevent migration to Europe—with more than questionable human rights consequences, as NGOs regularly point out.

2. Societies Confronted with an Upending Earth System

The issue of migration is intertwined with the massive ecological changes on Earth and leads us to the biggest change of the last 30 years. While it was long believed that Earth system science was exaggerating its warnings about anthropogenic global warming, it has become clearer with each passing year that the Earth has left the safe operating space for humanity. Three systems in particular have exceeded the planetary thresholds so clearly that the theory of tipping points was also confirmed empirically about 15 years ago. The loss of biodiversity, global warming, and disruptions of the nitrogen cycle have unleashed a dynamic of a magnitude that was not predicted by science. Tipping points, which unfolded abruptly as relatively sudden shifts after a long period of latency, have now fundamentally changed the Earth system. The previously prevailing idea that human societies write their history independently of natural history against the relatively stable backdrop of nature has become completely obsolete. However, the social sciences still struggle to reconfigure their analytical tools so that the entanglements of non-human ('natural') and human temporalities can be examined from a general ecological perspective. Accordingly, natural-scientific Earth-system research has long since advanced to become the leading scientific discipline.

CO_2 emissions were gradually reduced in the Global North. After the coronavirus crisis, the states regained their power to act, and a Green Deal reduced emissions in several countries in the Global North starting in 2022. Nevertheless, the successes of these emissions reductions were far from sufficient to meet the goal of limiting global warming to 1.5 to 2 degrees Celsius, which had been officially established as part of the Paris Agreement in 2015. In terms of *Realpolitik*, it was assumed even then that global warming would reach 3.5 to 4 degrees by the end of the 21st century. Joint climate policy decisions by the global community did not materialize, as carbon-driven countries such as the USA, Russia, Saudi Arabia, and other Gulf states repeatedly undermined collective regulations. Rebound effects and the growth of economies in the Global South combined with population growth (the world's population is currently around 9.5 billion people) did the rest. An ever-growing global middle class has driven a further increase in energy demand. In 2045, global warming reached 2 degrees, and it seems very likely that further warming will no longer be gradual but erratic and self-perpetuating. The current prediction is that the three-degree limit will be reached between 2065 and 2075. This will massively exacerbate the existing problems with the global water supply, and the areas that can be inhabited by humans will continue to shrink; further conflicts and wars are to come.

The securitization and militarization of climate policy has been increasing for 25 years. It is precisely the militarily, economically, and politically influential countries that are concerned with securing important resources such as energy, water, soil, and food. Some cities, on the other hand, have developed into green centers of sustainability and resilience (e.g., in Japan, Germany, Scandinavia, and Canada), in part through the use of AI and the digitalization of all areas of life. Many megacities in the Global South, however, regularly face infrastructural collapse owing to water shortages, heat waves, floods, and storms and use digital technologies as early warning systems and monitoring tools for entire population groups.

While the pros and cons of geoengineering measures were still being debated 30 years ago, they have now been an integral part of climate policy measures for around 25 years. It became clear that carbon-capture storage only helped to reduce CO_2 emissions to a limited extent. Thus, large-scale technological interventions in the Earth system began in 2031, partly spurred by massive protest from individual nations of the Global South. The fertilization of the oceans was stopped in 2042 in light of unforeseen feedback loops with the marine biochemical cycles. The discharge of aerosols into the Earth's atmosphere, despite the measurable reduction in solar radiation, also became highly controversial because of the massive feedback effects on atmospheric processes with strong weather fluctuations. Many social movements from the Global North and South are therefore now calling on politics, business, and science to abandon the hubris of wanting to steer the Earth system towards a 'good Anthropocene.' They refer to *The Second Convivialist Mani-*

festo, published in 2020, which generally denounces human hubris and instead pleads for self-limitation and conviviality among humans and non-humans alike.

3. World Politics

Political constellations are extremely different from region to region, which is also due to the fact that the model of Western modernity—forcefully supported first by European colonialism and then by the USA—is no longer recognized as generally binding. Even before the Trump administration, the US had abandoned its global political role as a hegemon that also provides global public goods. China has since risen to become a new global player with great political, military, and economic dominance but still shies away from taking responsibility for global commons. This, in turn, is also a result of internal conflict (e.g., democracy claims of the middle classes) for which the authoritarian country has not yet found any integrative answers.

Moreover, the three principles of order of the second half of the 20th century—that is, liberal democracy, free-market capitalism, and a pluralistic and individualistic culture, which lasted until the 2010s—are only robust and still alive in a few countries. They have come under increasing pressure from right-wing populist movements, and the counter-projects of authoritarian, illiberal nation states (coupled with notions of homogeneous communities) are in permanent conflict with defenders of individual liberties. The idea of human rights has also come under pressure from common-good-oriented, anti-individualist concepts of relational rationality (*tianxia* in Chinese).

In the last 20 years of ecological crisis, most nations have experienced both authoritarian phases of states of emergency and the disintegration or even collapse of established infrastructures as well as political and socio-economic orders. Capitalist enterprises in the 'crisis industry' such as security companies are profiting from this disintegration, and the economy of crisis (including state expenditure for crisis management and abatement) already accounts for 27 percent of the world's GDP.

4. Future Imaginaries

These developments have also contributed to change in the religious landscape, fed by the new social, economic, and ecological lines of conflict. Charismatic movements within the world religions became stronger. Various processes of sacralization have been observed: traditional revivals of collective sacralization in the form of nationalism or racism but also new immanent sacralities that regard Gaia, nature, or aspects of nature as sacred. The Earth, the cosmos—all these entities have been sacralized in the new age of the Anthropocene, and we are just experiencing the beginnings of this phenomenon. Most prominent and influential at present are collapsological notions that have been combined with apocalyptic ones. Advocates of such a perspective cultivate a religious narrative of an eschatologically necessary collapse that stands in the way of further efforts towards social-ecological transformation and habitability on Earth.

On the whole, our time is characterized by very contrasting processes, contradictions, conflicts, innovations, and normative regressions. In some places, we are falling far behind a basic level of civilization that we had achieved, whereas in others, new ideals of transformation are being advocated that can only to a very limited extent provide impulses for global society. In 2021, it became increasingly clear that the idea of modernization had merged with a control and security paradigm and that the path of radical social-ecological transformation aimed at a new post-capitalist beginning had only succeeded in social niches at the local or regional level.

What the future of the second half of the 21st century will bring is largely open, but this openness is far from the ideas that moderns once entertained about the future, ideas that—from today's perspective—seem based on almost naive beliefs in the notion of progress for all. It is precisely the extant belief that in principle anything can be accomplished, that organization and technology will overcome every limit, that has so far repeatedly led to the failure to build a convivialist politics of self-limitation and new beginnings as an alternative to the hubris of modernity. Political theorists of the 20th century like Hannah Arendt saw in the illusion of omnipotence, of being able to dominate man and nature, a totalitarian and destructive element, which, as we must note today, has not yet been overcome.

Once upon a Time ...
There Will Be a Convivial Desire
A Tale in Three Parts about the Possibility of Convivial Desire, Inspired (at the Beginning) by Saint Augustine's *De Trinitate*

Alain Caillé

First Tableau: Three Discourses of Desire

Saint Augustine, in his treatise *On the Trinity* (XIII.iii.6), tells the following story. At one time, a comic actor regularly traveled through the provinces of the Roman Empire. In each town, after finishing his performance, he announced to his audience, "Tonight I will reveal to you what you all desire. Let it be known, come in great numbers." And in the evening, indeed, a huge crowd of people came to hear him. "I know what you all want," the actor declared in a confident tone, as if he were drawing his knowledge from a sacred source, as mysterious as it was unquestionable. "You all want to buy cheap and sell dear." At these words, the entire crowd, delighted and dazzled by such penetrating insight, exclaimed: "Yes, that's right, that's exactly how it is. He has seen right through us."

But at the same time, in the same cities or elsewhere, another actor using the same procedure gave a different answer. "I know what you all want," he said to the crowd in a tone of voice as confident and inspired as his competitor's. "You all want to be praised and esteemed. You want to be loved, honored, and revered." At these words, the entire crowd, equally delighted and dazzled by his penetrating insight, exclaimed: "Yes, that's right, that's exactly how it is. He has seen right through us."

A third actor, who looked like a prophet, had something else to say:

"I have heard what the histrionics who roam your province tell you, deceiving you with their fine words and cunning arguments. Knowing that you all aspire to happiness—indeed, what else can one wish for?—they try to make you believe that you can achieve it by cheating your fellow man to buy the best deal possible and sell for more than you should. Or that you could find happiness by trying to win the good graces of the many through servile and degrading maneuvers. But who does not see that these answers are absurd and fallacious? If you deceive others, you will be deceived by them. And there is nothing more unstable and uncertain than popular favor. Praised and adored one day, you will be despised and reviled by all the next. No, truly, I say to you, the only way to be happy in an absolutely lasting and certain way is to place all your hopes and all your love in an all-powerful god."

In reality—and Augustine was the first to agree, estimating that there were more than two hundred different schools and definitions of happiness in antiquity—there was nothing new about these discourses. They had been around for a long time. What Augustine could not foresee, however, was their posterity. Over the course of the centuries, the followers of the first discourse, the discourse of economy and need, were to be found first among merchants and bankers, of course, and then among craftsmen and industrialists, and gradually spread to entire countries and states. Thanks to the refinements of economics, it is now robots with algorithms that buy at the lowest price and sell at the highest. They no longer buy goods or services, but money or promises of money, and they do so in a nanosecond, beyond all power of human reason or computation.

The descendants of the proponents of the second discourse, that of the desire for recognition, were recruited first and foremost among the warriors and aristocrats, ready to risk their lives for a noble cause—*God and kingdom*—or, more recklessly, quarrel over a simple point of honor.

Seeking glory—vainglory, their critics said—even in the cannon's mouth or in the slightest duel, triggered by a yes or a no, they claimed a monopoly on honor and recognition. Today, with this monopoly finally broken, everyone wants to be recognized. Everyone wants to be proud of their religion, their culture, their values, their sexuality, their gender, their country, their work, their unique personality. Everyone wants to be loved, respected, and valued. This discourse of desire and recognition is propagated by many philosophers, anthropologists, and psychoanalysts.

For centuries, and even millennia, however, merchants and warriors, champions of need as well as heroes of desire have affirmed at least in words the superiority in principle of the third discourse, the discourse of the gods and of love: the discourse of religion. In the realm of ideas, warriors and merchants gave way to priests, pontiffs, and prophets, even if the military and economic leaders still held sway over their religious counterparts when it came to wealth or the means of coercion. It was in the name of the gods that warriors fought, evoking the precepts of religion, even if they were often motivated only by the pleasure of fighting or the hope of finding glory or, more prosaically, the wealth that came from plunder. It was by giving the representatives of the gods enough to build churches, temples, mosques, pagodas, or cathedrals that merchants and bankers, for their part, hoped to find salvation for their souls.

For a good part of the twentieth century, it was believed that the discourse of religion was destined to die out little by little. That it would in any case desert the public square and exist only in private cults. Yet, at the beginning of the twenty-first century, it rose from its ashes, more alive than ever. Religious wars, thought to be from another time, are now back in the spotlight. And humanity wonders why.

Second Tableau: The End of Time?

Imagine, if you will, that we are now in the year 2030. Humanity is on the verge of despair. Countries that were once rich have fallen into misery and chaos. Others that were poor have become richer at first and then seen their development come to a halt. In any case, there are no longer enough sources of energy, oil, coal, and uranium and not enough raw materials to support sustainable growth. In many parts of the world, the air has become unbreathable at least every other day. Unemployment is rising disproportionately everywhere, because not only is there no need to hire in times of stagnation or recession, but many tasks can now be done better and more cheaply by robots—even tasks that were once considered skilled, middle-class tasks. While the rest of the world is in misery, a few million rich people, growing ever richer, live in tax havens, protected by high walls, barbed wire, dogs, and henchmen. They have to protect themselves against both the anger and hatred of all the social strata that have been demoted, and against the despair of the poor and climate refugees. The latter now number in the tens of millions or more since the melting of the ice pack has accelerated in the Arctic and Antarctic and the sea level has risen by almost one meter. With no one knowing what tomorrow will bring, more and more people are joining organized crime. Corruption reigns supreme everywhere.

Religions, for their part, are trying to preserve what they can of the sense of the common good, and attempting to defend the elementary rules of public and private morality. But they have difficulty convincing people because those who suffer from misery and fear are less and less sensitive to the promise of a paradise after death. If anything, they would prefer to enter a tax haven on Earth, and as soon as possible. Religions, which are supposed to preach peace, moderation, and love, are themselves dragged into this vortex and in turn become factors and amplifiers of the wars that set whole regions ablaze: Allah against God or YHWH, and vice versa. Buddha against Islam. Sunni Islam against Shiite Islam, in their many variants. And vice versa.

Faced with this disaster, voices are being raised all over the world and experiments are being devised to try to avert the catastrophe. Many avenues are being explored. In reality, everyone can see what should be done—at least in principle. First of all, we need to tackle the fantastic rise in inequality that has exploded all over the planet at an ever-increasing rate over the last fifty years. It is this inequality that fuels corruption and encourages organized crime. And, conversely, inequality feeds on it. How else could the richest people continue to earn 10–15 percent returns on their investments in sluggish or no-growth economies each year? But the end of growth is not the end of progress. It is only the end of the regular increase in the monetary purchasing power of market goods and services. It is possible to live better, infinitely better, in peace and security, without growth in monetary purchasing power, provided that it is better distributed and that the creativity of all is encouraged. Only then will it be possible to deal with global warming, the scarcity of energy and mineral resources, and the various forms of pollution and thus the wars and crimes that result from all these perturbations.

In 2030, everyone was firmly convinced of this. However, there was no sign of any progress or any possibility of a happy outcome to the world's dramatic disorders. No one knew what answer to give to a problem that everyone sensed was crucial but that no one could really name: the problem of the nature of human desire. What fuels it? Can it be controlled? Can it be or become convivial? Is it not, on the contrary, always doomed to excess, to boundlessness, to hubris? How can we reproach the richest people for wanting to become ever richer if we want the same things as they do? In whose name would we criticize the desire for recognition of great artists, exceptional sportsmen, writers, or brilliant scientists when we admire them and, in the field that we cherish, they serve as a model? We would like to be like them. And why should we denounce the religion or values of others when we know and understand them as poorly as they know and understand ours? Are they waging war on us? But can we be sure that we did not start it ourselves? No one knows when the war started or whether anything will ever stop it. It is true that all religions and all moralities have tried, but none has truly succeeded so far.

Third Tableau: The Symposium of Desire

Yet, the 857 speakers from all over the world who attended the so-called *Last Chance Congress* in the UN building, which at this point had been closed for five years, concluded that we have no choice. We must now solve the riddle of riddles once and for all and finally find out why, despite all their desire for peace and brotherhood, human beings always end up regressing into hatred and conflict. Where is the crack in their desire that sooner or later makes it turn against itself? If we do not learn to answer this question as soon as possible, humanity will perish. Morally, and perhaps even physically.

By a unanimous decision, the congress decided to convene nine representatives of each of the three discourses of desire that the congressmen had identified as the most relevant and plausible: the discourse of need and economy, the discourse of desire and recognition, and the discourse of gods and love.

The conditions imposed on the twenty-seven advocates were drastic. They were forced to live in Spartan accommodation and eat frugally, and they were forbidden to leave the house in which they were confined. They would only regain their freedom on the day when they unanimously agreed among themselves. If they could not agree, they could vote for one of the two other conceptions of desire. The one with the most votes would be declared the winner, and an attempt would be made to organize human coexistence on that basis.

As one might expect, for more than three months there was nothing but mockery, admonition, and quips exchanged between our twenty-seven heralds, each one pointing out the logical weaknesses and inconsistencies of the others or showing to what extent reality belied their initial hypotheses and conclusions. Day after day, unusual alliances were formed with a reversed front to defeat a common adversary, then undone the next day, only to be reversed the day after. Everyone, even within their own camp, was accused of bland idealism, narrow-minded materialism, silliness, misplaced empiricism, improbable transcendentalism, unjustifiable apriorism, unbearable cynicism, grotesque angelism, and so on. Never before had so much intelligence and subtlety been deployed to demonstrate the foolishness of others. The entire history of philosophy, social sciences, and religions was thus mobilized in a sort of endless agonistic joust. Everyone enjoyed it at first.

But no progress was made, and little by little the participants began to tire of these sterile exchanges. The hope of victory became more and more improbable, while the differences between them, which at first had seemed so immense, so irreconcilable, became more and more tenuous. On the one hundred and third day, an economist, a philosopher, and a religious figure who had raised the possibility while sipping insipid tea, proposed that a three-member commission take stock and outline a possible motion for a synthesis. Their proposal was greeted with general relief, and they were immediately elected to the committee. So many arguments had been exchanged during these three months, so many in-depth discussions had taken place, that they were only half surprised to come to an agreement in a few days on three sets of proposals, which can be summarized as follows:

- First of all, there is no absolute choice to make between the three opposing conceptions of desire. Each one encompasses and interprets the other two, and each one is interpreted and encompassed by them. Beyond the narrow sphere of need, it is the desire to be recognized and the desire to fulfill one's religious obligations (or demand for meaning) that fuels the desire for possession. Likewise, one cannot be recognized without receiving a quantity of goods that crystallizes this recognition, and one is never recognized, in the end, except in proportion to what one has given or what one could give. Finally, obedience to the gods and to ultimate values only makes sense if it allows each person to obtain the quantity of goods necessary for his or her existence and to enjoy the recognition of his or her uniqueness.
- Moreover, the modalities of desire vary according to the individual. This is why there can be no general theory of desire that is valid a priori for everyone. But what we absolutely need is not a general theory of desire but a clear distinction between legitimate and illegitimate desires. Not all desires are admissible, and those humans

who fall prey to them must learn to not yield to the deleterious part of their desire. Legitimate are those desires whose expression allows humans to live and cooperate in opposition without slaughtering each other.
- Legitimate, then, is the desire for possession that does not turn into a *pleonexia*, a desire to have more and more. Legitimate is the desire for recognition that does not turn into *hubris*, into a desire to escape the human condition and common humanity. The love of the gods is legitimate as long it is not transformed into hatred of men and the world.

Standing in front of the other twenty-four delegates once again, the economist, the philosopher, and the religious man presented these three sets of proposals, explaining how and why they had arrived at them. They were unanimously accepted. And it was also unanimously decided to call the doctrine that made it possible to bring these three proposals together in a coherent way *convivialism*, the art of living together.

The three proposals were not made public immediately. It was considered preferable to write a whole series of preambles and explanations beforehand, if only to show that they had worked well. So it was not until ten days later that white smoke rose from the main chimney of the house. It meant:

> "We have a doctrine. A doctrine that can be shared by all human beings of good will. We know which way to go. Everyone can join in according to their own history and their own beliefs, as long as they are aware that the future of humanity and the survival of the planet are at stake and that there is no more pressing need than to learn to coexist by opposing each other without slaughtering each other."

The news spread like wildfire throughout the world. Soon everyone was eager to adopt the symbol of the new world view and work towards its realization. Many of the very wealthy, who had been waiting for this very moment, soon joined in. Just as quickly, yielding to corruption seemed dishonorable. It took a little longer for the soldiers of the warring armies and the members of the criminal gangs to begin to abandon them; but once the movement had begun, it gained increasing momentum and nothing could stop it. There was so much else to do: to invent a world of convivial prosperity without systematic GDP growth and to heal all the world's ills inherited from past centuries. Finally, it goes without saying that throughout the world, men and women of all colors and religions married or partnered. And they had many children. But not too many.

A Reflection on 200 Years of Our Youngest Bodily Organ—*Convivialis Futuris*

Susanne Bosch et al.[1]

> Future generations will look back at the epochal transition we are making to a life-sustaining society. And they may well call this the time of the Great Turning. It is happening now ... The Great Turning is a name for the essential adventure of our time: the shift from the Industrial Growth Society to a life-sustaining civilization.
> (Joanna Macy, 2009)

---

1 The conceptual setting was developed by Susanne Bosch and put into practice in a conversation lasting three hours on April 11, 2021, together with: Dr. Herman Bashiron Mendolicchio (researcher, curator, lecturer), Dr. Susanne Bosch (artist, artistic researcher), Aje Brücken (script writer, coach), Niamh DeLoughry (humanitarian and development worker, Deputy Chief Executive at Royal Dublin Society), Dr. Angela Dreßler (ethnographer and artistic researcher, büro eta boeklund), Siri Frech (landscape architect, urbanist, process facilitator), Christina Jacoby (art mediator, exhibition production manager), Tellervo Kalleinen (artist, musician, acupuncturist), Prof. Dr. Elke Krasny (cultural theorist, curator, urbanist and author), Sahar Qawasami (architect, architect restorer, planner, and cultural heritage expert, curator, writer, co-founder and director of Sakiya), and Jeffrey Tan (theatre director, creative producer, drama educator). This text was inspired by many things but chiefly by Elke Krasny, Lena Fritsch, Sophie Lingg, and Claudia Lomoschitz and their organ-based collective writing process "I KNOW, I (Self-) CARE. TAKING BACK SELF CARE" on February 4, 2021 (online), and by an exercise developed by Joanna Macy, called "7th Generation" (also called "The Double Circle") as part of her "Work that Reconnects." Susanne Bosch wants to thank everyone involved for the inspiring and generous contri-

1. From Today's Perspective in 2221

A virus that globally appeared around late 2019–early 2020 (called coronavirus or COVID-19), tipped the long-predicted simmering peak of the industrial growth society, facing a social, economic, political, environmental and climate change. The shift came through collapse and turmoil, not through a disaster-free moment of designing our future. Everything long predicted happened very quickly from 2020 onwards, as we had reached various tipping points by then. It also led to a transformative change in our bodies and subsequently our minds.

It turned out that the virus started the evolutionary process of growing a new bodily organ. Yes, from today's perspective in 2221, it seems unimaginable that we as a human species did not have this internal and external organ all along. Indeed, this extremely sensory organ with the medical name *convivialis futuris* (today conventionally known as *CF*) started to slowly grow from 2020.

In 2021–22, *CF* was detected and from then onwards carefully observed and monitored. At first, scientists thought this would be the end of the human species with unknown and uncontrollable extra tissue growing in everyone's body. COVID-19 was a contagious disease with zoonotic origin: hidden cellular information that jumped from the animal and plant world to the human one.

Back then, we humans separated ourselves from plants, animals, and other living beings. We defined ourselves as different, believing only humans had a consciousness and the ability to think and therefore freely decide. Little did we understand, back then, of the compassion and need for interconnectedness, but this revolutionary moment of our ancestors became the starting point of everything that we as present-day beings live and represent.

In 2021, scientists only slowly started to understand that the human body is made of symbiotic material. It takes the form of great biodi-

---

butions. Many thanks especially to Ulrike Zimmermann, Angela Dressler, and Steve Tiller for their editorial input.

versity between bacteria, virus, micro-organism, and fungi, all living in peaceful coexistence within the human body. Philosopher Timothy Morton, referring to Donna Haraway, asserted that human beings are cyborgs of a kind, since we are made up of all sorts of non-human components. Our DNA contains a significant amount of genetic material from others.

2. A Global Meeting of Delegates beyond Chronological Time

To explore and specify the qualities of the *CF*, five living beings from 2221 met five ancestors from 2021, the generation that was first introduced to COVID-19, and subsequently the bodily organ. Their meeting alternated between one-on-one interviews, reflections, and group sessions. Twice they all spoke intimately in pairs and twice they all met listening to the outcomes of these conversations. Such as a trial of how to understand one's present.

This text is a report of such an encounter. Ten delegates speaking from different global locations, this being their place of origin, place of choice or place of existence. Some of these places have vanished in 2221, some still exist or have been newly formed. The delegates' words reveal perspectives in various cultural, geographical, social, and political contexts and, of course, in time. Summed up in this report one will find the most crucial findings and musings of this encounter. Each part of the following centers around specific aspects and sheds a light on perceptions each of the two generations bear in mind. It is strongly informed by the ancestor's keen interest to learn about the bodily organ, its shape and function, and thus, life 200 years after the *CF* first developed. And though *CF* clearly enables time travel, yet these types of concentrated exchanges are rare and obviously less familiar for the present ancestors.

The ancestor Herman Bashiron Mendolicchio, from Barcelona, former Spain, met with Christina Jacoby, from Bregenz, former Austria. Ancestor Elke Krasny, from Vienna/Austria met Niamh DeLoughry, from the Wicklow Mountains, formerly Ireland. Jeffrey Tan, from a place formerly known as Singapore, spoke with ancestor Angela

Dressler, from former Berlin. Tellervo Kalleinen, from former Helsinki in Finland, conversed with Aje Brücken, an ancestor from Berlin/Germany. Finally, Siri Frech, from former Berlin, talked to ancestor Sahar Qawasmi, from former Ramallah/Palestine.

3. *Convivialis Futuris* (*CF*) and Its Sensory Abilities

It came as a blunt surprise to many of the ancestors, that humankind was still alive and mostly well in 2221 and indeed, the curiosity to understand life with and without *CF* became the driving force of the following conversations. We are still living as biological beings in the circle of life and death, here with our delicate and precious bodies.

Its Shape

The five future delegates described shape and functions of their organs in detail. First of all, ancestors had to understand not all organs were alike nor perfectly equal in their functions. In the former Singaporean area, only old people with life experience—and not all of them—, are experiencing the growth of an external bodily organ on their forehead. In many Asian religions as Buddhism, Hinduism, Zen and Taoism, this special sensory function was historically titled the *third eye*. The third eye provides a perception beyond ordinary sight. It is said to allow humans to tune into the correct *vibration* of the universe. Delegate Jeffrey pointed out that wearing facial masks for 200 years and all the time made the eyes in general become more expressive and communicative: the eyes of compassion, the eyes of understanding, the eyes of being there, the eyes of resilience, the eyes of mutual observation, the eyes of honoring nature and reclaiming land that was destroyed.

Tunar, a being from the former North of Europe, described the *CF* of that region in great detail to her partner. It is called Wing Brain. It is located in the neck around the C7 vortex, at the lowest end of it. It merges with the spinal column and goes up on the back of the head, where it divides into two wing-like shapes. It serves as a connector between the outer body and our nervous system. The external and internal organ is very sensitive to different kinds of resonances and can feel the effect of actions. It reads information in a non-verbal way. It is a parallel system where information is not filtered through our brain. In daily life, people can consciously tune in to either their rational mind or their Wing Brain.

Siri from former Germany described her external and internal organ, located also in the neck around the C7 vortex, to ancestor Sahar like this: "It is a kind of impulse bodily organ more directed to the outside. It connects your inner impulse to the multiple impulses around you. It connects to the vibrating impulse that all living beings have: plants, animals, and minerals. We can connect to their difference sequences. It gives us energy. It is nutritious."

The bodily organs in Middle Europe (former Austria and Ireland) are located in the front of the body, close to the heart on the chest. Christina:

> "The bodily organ has the external shape of a flower. It can be open or closed. It can perceive, on the one hand, the inner landscape and be in connection with all the other internal organs in my body. And on the other hand, it can be open to the outside world and connect with other living beings. It is primarily a sensory organ of perception. What is special: I can cultivate and decide to be on the outside or focus on the inside so that I can be more connected or focused on myself."

Niamh described her external CF on the chest, covered when not wanting to expose what you are feeling as it changes in color depending on what it is that one is feeling deficient in. When government representatives are coming together it is obligatory to make it visible so that there is full transparency over the aim to serve societal needs over capital gains.

Its Function

The CF, as third eye, allows the elders to experience a kind of *tuning in*. They are not afraid to try things they have never done before. The

CF gives them courage, energy, and a feeling of connecting physically and emotionally. They feel very positive, and are recognized by their smiling faces and creative instincts. Delegate Jeffrey cautions, however, that having the CF does not transform you. It's a passport or a fuel that allows you to connect with somebody else; to interact with other people, bringing like-minded people together. Jeffrey expressed the wish to grow older quicker to experience this.

The Wing Brain amplifies instinctive or intuitive impulses, making them clearer, and promoting our intuition. The evolved Wing Brain is not confused by biased thought, rather retains precision, clarity, and sophistication. The Wing Brains are communicating between each other. Until today, we do not know exactly what they communicate. The ethos of the connected Wing Brain is the wellbeing of all through collective, instinctive wisdom.

Siri added that the CF allows to relax deeply so one feels these impulses and connections all the time. From this state of deep relaxation, one interacts with others. The neck area is the most relaxed and connected zone of the human body. The front and back of our body both sense the world.

Christina described how the day with her flower-shaped CF starts: "The CF makes a kind of 'proposal' in the morning. It gives an impulse. I can consciously open or close it. During the day, from time to time, I receive an impulse that feels like a small tickle. It reminds me that I can decide to be listening, feeling, and perceiving outwards or inwards."

The CF regulates and balances body, mind, spirit, and emotions.

Grief is the original *driver* of the CF that Niamh described to ancestor Elke: "COVID-19 caused so many deaths. It reminded us how precious life is." Regardless of socioeconomic status or nationality, sexual orientation or whatever markers humans were pigeonholed with in 2021, nowadays the CF connects us. Helps us see each other's common humanity and everyone's basic needs. It also helps us connect with the environment and with climate, ensuring a fair and equitable world, whatever global policies are in place. The CF functions in two parts. Part one is about the individual feelings. Part two is foregrounding the surrounding environment and reacting to its needs and our responsibilities as well as contributions.

4. Life & Death and the Presence of Time

People are still being born, grow up and die. In former Singapore, what has changed in 200 years is the fact that people work less, on the level of retired people in 2021. They have less stress and spend time with things that are important to them such as nature and family. As there is close to no travel movement possible due to the mutated virus, borders stopped to exist.

In 2021, research found out that the nervous system stays awake for still some time after death. The Wing Brain actually stays active years after death. It very slowly decomposes. The decomposed soil still holds some kind of consciousness and awareness for hundreds of years after death. We are growing food in this soil. The food carries parts of this awareness. In 2021, there was an obvious learning blockage. Intellectual knowledge and experimental wisdom did not make humans arrive at new practices. Rather, a lot of emotional trauma through experience blocked the awareness even more. The Wing Brain is answering this problem through cultivating awareness. Every generation is arriving already with certain insights. All are surrounded by and fed from Wing Brain soil. Everyone has a Wing Brain. Depression, a long-lasting pandemic in former centuries, has disappeared. Feelings of isolation, struggling for love and attention are unknown. Instead, to exploring one's own self and life is more connected to the feeling of curiosity. Oneself and others are not two separate things. Belonging is not a struggle anymore. Everyone can have strong encounters with others because the Wing Brains are resonating with many people and places. Being in strong resonance is not questioned nor problematic.

Siri explained that time is a constant rhythm and not being counted. We live still in our bodies and in a specific place, but we can connect to everybody everywhere:

> "It is still wonderful to see different places. We still travel with our physical bodies. But we travel a lot with our organ. If I want to connect to somebody in another place, I use the CF. A good friend might be somewhere else, but I don't feel disconnected. There is no feeling of being apart because of space. Borders therefore don't have any use anymore. We don't have them anymore." Siri admits: "We are really open to change and live in/with constant change. We lost the fear of change. Not completely, to be honest, but there is trust in life. We know of its complexity and we physically feel we are part of it."

In death, the personal impulse does not stop being an impulse, it just changes the condition: "When we die, we are still connected in this kind of impulse network. We won't fall out of it."

Christina pointed out that we are no longer familiar with many former diseases like *burn-out* because the CF reacts and regulates swiftly. The bodily CF organ does not require us to think about our needs or the needs of the ecosystem, but helps us perceive the need for balance. Herman, the enquiring ancestor, called this quality peace, harmony, beauty, and love. Christina left it open, as all correctly express the qualities of living beings. Work as such does not exist anymore. Work is about creating situations. Things now happen in a more fluid and organic space with no timetable. Christina describes life as a cycle of rising and growing until, step by step, we let life leave the body to become part of the body of the bigger Earth. In death, the CF is balancing the mental, emotional, and physical process. Emotions like joy and sorrow are part of being human and welcomed. As a regular traveler in time, Christina knows: "We have a lot of states of the mind you don't have. Everybody has individual mind states here. We enjoy diversity."

Niamh introduced a world in 2221 that no longer feels time-poor:

> "To be more connected means that we are able to ensure people can have a better balanced, more rounded life so that there is more time to do everything it takes to live that life. There are enough hours in the day to cook healthy meals, perhaps from your garden or your community garden. And there is enough time to experience nature regardless of the weather. There is enough time to still work and earn enough to

have a standard of living that is more equal. The organ helps to ensure that the policies in place are allowing for that more all-round life. There is still a need for economic sustainability. But that has been reduced by the recognition of the increased need for more time in the day to be more balanced."

As *CF* it triggers being grounded and fully in the moment. All lives are now fully intentional and fully present. By being more present with a quieter mind allows to be more productive as human beings, because we are engaging 100 percent with our mind and body. Elke was fascinated to find out that the new layers of sensitivity express themselves in words, as well as in feelings and bodily sensations.

5. Interim

Along the intimate exchanges around these astonishing insights, a number of general questions came up. One might be summarized as the great question of knowing: Do people in 2221 know more about the great mystery of life? It became clear that despite the *CF*'s workings, future people do not necessarily know about life's mysteries in full but that they seem to live in greater appreciation of the offerings of not-knowing. Delegate Jeffrey used the term "fluid Milky Way of things coming and going" and delegate Siri paraphrased it as trusting complexity:

> "It's more like you stand in front of wonderful art piece and you feel touched. You will never get to its ground, what is there and what you are able to feel, to see and to connect to. You will never understand your own complexity. It is even more basic: You can't understand. It allows for this openness to accept: I just can't see it, I can't hold it, but it's beautiful because it's so big."

Further questions informed by the realities in 2021 came up. One of the ancestors, Elke, wondered about legal and illegal organ trade markets. Was there such thing in 2221? We as future beings promptly clarified the impossibility to steal or transplant the organ and reinforced the thought of any wellbeing be less individualized but rather collective for us. The Wing Brains for example are interconnected on the basis of the collective wellbeing. The *CFs* would send strong impulses in case of any act against the wellbeing of this network. Jeffrey pointed out that the third eye is not something that one could manufacture. The *CF* is not an object. He phrased it as an almost mysterious gift or passport that can only work when all the elements come together. Taking it off someone who has passed away would also not work. Should a *CF* signal a malfunction through its color and shape, there is expertise to recognize its signal and try to heal it.

In summary, the ancestors saw all the organs working on a different level of connectedness, almost on a global one and resisted the globalized economy that existed in 2021. Ancestor Elke summarized: "The world that my future being shared with me was not at all an ideal world. It was still a very brutal world. The *CF* organ makes people feel more intensely and therefore makes it more difficult to conceal the existing injustices." Concerning the depiction of rather positive effects of the *convivialis futuris* workings, ancestral delegates like Sahar started wondering about inherent geopolitical settings. Are they still existing in our times, like the East–West or North–South epistemologies? And didn't all these descriptions mirror well-known narratives of progress in some areas of the world and dystopias in others?

6. Resources, Distribution, Consumption, and Survival

In order to enhance the mutual understanding, the situation of and around life-securing resources in 2221 as well as distribution, consumption and survival needed more detailed description, also befitting the need to position the role of the organ.

Compared to 2021, our life in 2221 seems more simplistic: Communities, be it cities, villages, or towns, strongly depend on local food and material production with due effects on diet as well as housing. Global economy as such is based on circular economies, re- and upcycling as well as renewable energies. We still experience the impact of the resource overuse in the early 21st century as huge burden. In response to this, we in 2221 rely on shorter productions chains and less good traffic, however modern technologies such as 3D printing allow universal knowledge to be translated into production onsite. In some geographical areas, the supply of external goods is still necessary. People nowadays enjoy the lightness of simplicity and non-possession.

Quite naturally ancestors inquired about the possibility to balance needs and consumption and individual desires. In general, many of us 2221'ers pointed out that work as such does not exist in the old form anymore and things happen in a more fluid, organic pace without timetables, making space to create instead. In places like Singapore everyday life was characterized by less work and less stress, meeting a lower living standard due to the 21st centuries turmoils and a persisting scarcity of resources. Nowadays we address this with more time to spend with 'what matters to people,' e. g. nature and family, as well as general forms of community building or urban gardening, planting trees and crop. Fostered by the elders' knowledge about what is essential, people are living less segregated, too.

The Wing Brain has helped to develop an advanced form of artificial intelligence. In 2021, artificial intelligence was about algorithms with a very problematic bias as it was developed and programmed by the human intelligence with bias tendencies. This next generation of artificial intelligence takes care to be connected with everything globally and makes sure that the basic things are distributed equally.

Siri described the spatial proximity in order to be more mindful with our resources. She also highlighted how we are able to live together in bigger groups and therefore bigger open spaces as we are not afraid of each other nor of intimacy with many. The urge to travel and move a lot has decreased massively as we experience ongoing connectedness. "The CF helps to always stay connected with oneself and with this resource to connect to the others. There is more openness for complexity and not knowing. We are not afraid of the complexity of other people. To be closer helps to share and to create."

Christina's description mirrors the absence of fear and the certain knowledge there is enough for everybody. Everyone takes what one needs and not more. The *CF* senses when it is enough.

In former Middle Europe, there is still a need to work and the need for a degree of production. Niamh highlighted there is still a language of concern. There continues to be religion and some governments that want to push against the global system. But there is a much more conscious awakening that wealth is not just about money and material gain. Investments are continuously being made to reduce mental and physical health issues caused by overabundance. The *CF* organ is increasing everybody's individual level of responsibility and awareness over the knock-on effect of every action. Mental and physical wellbeing are as important as money. The rising level of individual responsibility extends to a different type of resourcefulness or resource ethic.

> Niamh: "Our *CF* has evolved to ensure that our countries and our governments are working together to create an equitable balance, recognizing diversity of culture, religion, language, climate. There is not one model for all, but there is a minimum standard that we are living with today that ensures that all human beings do have more balance in their life, a wellbeing valued as much as economic wellbeing or financial stability. Distress and depression have been off-set by our *CF*, ensuring more time is available for being with nature, eating well and contributing to one's immediate community."

In 2221, there are banks not only for money, but for wellbeing. The banks manage the re-distribution of resources to ensure that all people have access to a minimum standard of wellbeing.

7. Ending Transcendental Homelessness

What became evident in the exchange between all delegates were the *CF*'s many similarities through geographical contexts, chiefly its impacts on becoming social. To imagine ways of living in ethical, political, and social terms from the perspective of the youngest bodily organ seemed alien to the ancestors. For us future beings, in retrospect, our CF organs provide for a greater sense of compassion and social sensing, social interdependence, interconnectedness and interrelatedness and foster reflections as much as insights. Some of the ancestors mused towards the end of the conversation, if some of this CF's knowledge might be much older, but overseen or overwritten. As future delegate Niamh responded, also referring to the setting of the conversation, that perhaps "in that respect, it is flipping the learning: We have a lot to learn from them. We are lagging so far behind the propositions they are giving to us."

Ancestor Herman reflected upon power and control, which our CF organ has not solved up to this point. The CF augmented—and is still augmenting—the sensitivity to approach these goals of heightened global social awareness: "If the CF controls the individual storms that we have, then the other global storms, the global systems, the brutality of the systems, should be automatically controlled as well."

As our form of existence is so common and well known to ourselves, the ten delegates speaking helps us understand better our collective, as well as individual purpose, in the context of time.

List of Contributors

Frank Adloff is a Professor of Sociology at the University of Hamburg where he also is the co-director of the Humanities Centre for Advanced Studies "Futures of Sustainability." He is chairperson of the International Convivialist Association.

Christian Arnsperger, PhD in economics, is a Professor of Sustainability at the University of Lausanne, where he conducts research on post-capitalism, post-consumerism, economic anthropology, and ecological monetary theory.

Geneviève Azam is an essayist; she was attached as an economist to the University Jean Jaurès in Toulouse; she is involved in Attac-France and in the climate and ecologist movement.

Susanne Bosch (Dr.) is an interface activist, an artist and artist researcher. For her, art is a practice for entering into dialogue about social, political, and historical events as well as an interface where, through/with aesthetic forms, a different way of dealing with given conditions can be tested. As an "interface activist," she works on long-term questions that deal with concepts of democracy and sustainable futures.

Tanja Busse is a moderator and author living in Hamburg. She published *Das Sterben der anderen* ("The Dying of the Others") on the loss of biodiversity in 2019.

Alain Caillé is a Professor Emeritus of Sociology at the University of Paris-Ouest Nanterre and founder of the MAUSS and the convivialist movement.

Sérgio Costa is a Professor of Sociology at Freie Universität Berlin and co-director of the Maria Sibylla Merian Centre Conviviality-Inequality in Latin America (Mecila).

Thomas Coutrot is an economist at Dares, the research centre of the French Ministry of labour; he authored several books on the issues of work, health and democracy.

Federico Demaria is an Assistant Professor of Ecological Economics and Political Ecology at the University of Barcelona, and a fellow at the Humanities Centre for Advanced Studies "Futures of Sustainability." He has co-edited *Degrowth* (2014), *Pluriverse* (2019), and co-authored *The Case for Degrowth* (2020).

Jonathan DeVore is an Academic Counsel (*Akademischer Rat auf Lebenszeit*) with the Department of Social and Cultural Anthropology at the University of Cologne in Germany. He has been conducting ethnographic and ethnohistorical research in North-Eastern Brazil since 2002, and received his PhD from the University of Michigan in 2014.

Matthias Fersterer co-founded the magazine "Oya—enkeltauglich leben" and runs the independent publishing press "Drachen Verlag." He lives in Klein Jasedow in North-East Germany in one of the country's longest standing intentional communities.

Eric Hirsch is an Assistant Professor of Environmental Studies at Franklin and Marshall College, Pennsylvania, whose research focuses on the relationship between environmental change, economic development, and how marginalized communities build their livelihoods. He is the author of the forthcoming book *Acts of Growth: Development and the Politics of Abundance in Peru*.

The International ECG Movement started 2010 in Vienna and has spread to 33 countries since. It aims at developing an economy that is oriented towards the common good.

Ashish Kothari is a co-founder of Kalpavriksh and Vikalp Sangam in India, and the Global Tapestry of Alternatives; he is a co-editor of *Alternative Futures: India Unshackled,* and *Pluriverse: A Post-Development Dictionary.*

Robert van Krieken is a Professor Emeritus of Sociology at The University of Sydney, as well as an Adjunct Professor at University College, Dublin, and the University of Tasmania.

Martin Krygier is a Professor of Law and Social Theory, Faculty of Law & Justice, University of New South Wales, Honorary Professor, Regulatory Institutions Network, Australian National University, and Senior Research Fellow, Democracy Institute, Central European University.

Paulo Henrique Martins is a Professor of Sociology at the Federal University of Pernambuco (Brazil) and former president of the Latin American Sociological Association (ALAS).

Gustave Massiah is an alterglobalist economist and is member of the International Council of the World Social Forum.

Dominique Méda is a Professor of Sociology at the University of Paris Dauphine-PSL where she also is the director of the institute for interdisciplinary research in the social sciences.

Solène Morvant-Roux is an Assistant Professor at the University of Geneva, funded by a grant from the Swiss National Research Foundation. She is the Principal Investigator of several research projects on financialization through debt in rural Mexico and in Switzerland and on alternative financial systems.

Débora Nunes is a Professor of Urbanism at the Bahia State University, Brazil, and is also founder and coordinator of the Integral Ecology School.

Susan Paulson is a Professor at the University of Florida's Center for Latin American Studies, where her ongoing exploration of human-environment relations draws on experiences from 15 years living among communities in Latin America, and five years teaching sustainability studies in Europe.

Elena Pulcini (†) was a Professor of Social Philosophy at the University of Florence, a public intellectual and committed convivialist. In her works, she focused on modern subjectivity, feminism, passions, and care. Her last book publication is *Tra Cura e Giustizia: Le Passioni come Risorsa Sociale* (2020; "Between Care and Justice: Passions as a Social Resource").

Jean-Michel Servet, a socio-economist, is a Professor Emeritus of Development Studies at the Graduate Institute in Geneva. He has been doing research on money and finance since the 1970s, in various countries as well as within the history of economic thought.

André Tiran is a Professor Emeritus of Economics at the Université Lumière Lyon-2. He is the coordinator of the complete works of Jean-Baptiste Say and conducts research on monetary theories from the 16th to the 18th century.

Andrea Vetter is a transition researcher, teaching Transformation Design at Braunschweig University of Art. She is co-creator and founder of the post-local art and transformation hub "Haus des Wandels" in Brandenburg (Germany).

Frank Adloff, Volker M. Heins (Hg.)
Konvivialismus. Eine Debatte

2015, 264 Seiten, kart., 19,99 €,
ISBN 978-3-8376-3184-5, E-Book: 17,99 €

Wo liegen die Stärken, wo die Schwächen des Konvivialismus? Was hieße es, eine konviviale Gesellschaft anzuvisieren – in Politik, Kultur und Wirtschaft? Mit Beiträgen u.a. von Micha Brumlik, Christian Felber, Naika Foroutan, Silke Helfrich, Claus Leggewie, Stephan Lessenich, Steffen Mau, Franz Walter und Gesa Ziemer.

BLOG zum Buch: https://blog.transcript-verlag.de/kategorie/konvivialismus

»Ein kritisches Echo des Manifests.« *Alex Capistran, Oya, 5/6 (2016)*

Die konvivialistische Internationale
Das zweite konvivialistische Manifest
Für eine post-neoliberale Welt

2020, 144 Seiten, 10,00 €, ISBN 978-3-8376-5365-6,
E-Book: Open Access

Das zweite konvivialistische Manifest legt die Grundlagen für ein Zusammenleben nach dem Neoliberalismus jenseits der menschlichen Hybris. Nach einer intensiven Diskussion haben fast 300 Wissenschaftler*innen, Intellektuelle und Aktivist*innen aus 33 Ländern dieses Manifest unterzeichnet.

BLOG zum Buch: https://blog.transcript-verlag.de/kategorie/konvivialismus

»[Das Buch ist] wertvoll und wichtig zugleich und es gibt auch und gerade während der Corona-Pandemie genügend Gründe, es zu lesen.«
Thomas Feltes, https://polizei-newsletter.de, 14.09.2020